AUGUST STRINDBERG

August Strindberg

An Introduction to his Major Works
by
BIRGITTA STEENE
University of Washington

ALMQVIST & WIKSELL INTERNATIONAL
Stockholm — Sweden
in collaboration with
HUMANITIES PRESS INC
N.J., — USA

Published in Sweden 1982 by
Almqvist & Wiksell International, Stockholm
in collaboration with
Humanities Press, Inc., Atlantic Higlands,
NJ 07716 USA
ISBN

Second Revised Edition of
The Greatest Fire. A Study of August Strindberg
published in 1973 by Southern Illinois University Press

Printed in Sweden 1982 by Graphic Systems AB

Introduction

Playwright, novelist, poet, and scientist, August Strindberg (1849–1912) was a conflict-ridden man who took all knowledge and experience that befell on him as his creative domain. Though hesitant at first about his career in life, he seems in retrospect like the embodiment of the professional poet who only deviated from the path of penmanship when the still more glorious adventures of scientist and alchemist beckoned him.

Strindberg was a prolific writer. The new national edition of his collected works will comprise some seventy-two volumes of dramas, novels, short stories, poetry, essays and diaries. It would be impossible to discuss within the scope of this volume Strindberg's production in its entirety without resorting to a mere cataloguing of the material. I have chosen to concentrate more fully on what I consider Strindberg's major works, and I have omitted from discussion all of his scientific and nonliterary writings, even though I feel that the time has come for a more thorough examination of Strindberg's ventures into journalism. But this book is designed as an introduction to August Strindberg. It attempts to moderate earlier biographical and psychological studies of him. The emphasis is on Strindberg the conscious artist and form-giver.

The religious and psychological crisis that Strindberg went through in the mid-nineties, which goes under the name of the Inferno period, was no doubt the most crucial event in his personal and creative life; and the customary division of his works into two periods using the Inferno upheavals as a watershed might seem well justified. The first period stretches from 1869 to 1890, the other from 1896 to the end of Strindberg's life in 1912. But such a chronological two-step method has often resulted in an oversimplified classification of Strindberg's works into two major categories: the Naturalistic works during the pre-Inferno years and the Expressionistic works in the post-Inferno period. The approach can easily lead the student to ignore the fact that Strindberg employed a panoramic stage and a kaleidioscopic dramatic presentation not only in *A Dreamplay* (1901) but in several dramas from his early career, such as *Lucky-Per's Journey* and *Keys of Heaven*; that he wrote fiction in the 1880's which anticipated the "Inferno vision" of life, for instance *The Sexton On Rånö* and *On the Seaboard*; that the years between the publication of such expressionistic works as *To Damascus* and *A Dreamplay* (1898–1901) also saw the birth of several of Strindberg's history plays, a genre that leads the thought back to his very first work for the stage, *Master Olof* (1872)

In his recent Strindberg biography, Olof Lagercrantz argues against interpreting the Inferno Crisis as a decisive change in Strindberg's approach to his art. Reiterating more forcefully what American Strindberg scholars like Erik Johannesson and Evert Springchorn had said before him, Lagercrantz maintains that Strindberg was throughout his life a self-experimentor who consciously staged his own personal dramas of jealousy, paranoia and misogyny, to be used as material in his literary works. Seen in such a context, the Inferno crisis is only one of many self-styled upheavals in Strindberg's life, reflected in his works.

As I suggest in my introductory chapter, Strindberg cultivated the role of the artist as homunculus, a Romantic idea embraced by such different writers as Keats, Chechov and Ibsen, who all suggested that the poetic personality had no real private identity but possessed the unique talent (and fateful weakness) of being able to absorb other people's selves into its own creative psyche. This notion of the artist as a kind of lamia is perhaps not in contradiction to the idea of the artist as a self-conscious and detached "meta-writer" who deliberately uses himself as a psychological guinea pig and subject for his art; for his inspiration the artist can, like some creative "schizophrenic", prey on his fragmented self as well as on other people.

To make Strindberg the cool observant of a dramatized personal life of his own making is an obvious attempt to refute the more traditional view of him as an uncontrolled exhibitionist and victim of emotional crises who unashamedly used art as self-therapy and, in the words of George Steiner, as "a mirror to the private soul". Yet, the problem with carrying the conception of Strindberg as a controlled self-experimentor too far is that it threatens to rob him of his individual uniqueness and reduces him to the artist as transcendent impersonal singer, a notion he himself came to propagate; it tempts us to obliterate from our mind the unmistakeable fact that Strindberg remained all his life a very vulnerable person, an oversensitive lover, and a suffering man. Though I wish to emphasize his writings over his private life, I would not want the Strindberg who emerges from these pages to be a kind of clever psychological con-artist with his pen.

For I believe that his work can only live on if we sense in them a person who has lived through and has genuinely felt a deeply tormented but truly human life.

Although the approach of this study is by and large chronological, the works have been grouped according to genre, which means that a strict year-by-year chronology has not always been maintained. There is also a separate chapter dealing with Strindberg's poetry, which spans a great part of his life but which has usually been completely ignored in discussions of Strindberg in English. The book is designed in such a way as to provide the reader with a view of Strindberg's development as an artist and at the same time make it easier for him to assess Strindberg's role within each literary type.

I wish to thank professor emeritus Walter Johnson for encouraging me to write this book and my colleagues and students over the years in the United States for many valuable discussions. I also wish to thank *Comparative Literature* for permission to use parts of an article I wrote on Strindberg's history plays, which appeared in CL, 11. No. 3 (1959).

University of Washington   BIRGITTA STEENE
February 1982

1

A Note on Strindberg
The Self and the Artist

It was August Strindberg who put into common Swedish usage the word *underklass*—recently translated by sociologist Gunnar Myrdal in reference to Negro slum inhabitants in the United States—to designate people living in the substrata of an industrial society. Nowadays the word, and its antonym *överklass*, is such an integral part of the Swedish language that few Swedes realize that these terms, like much of their daily idiom, can be led back to the linguistic revolution wrought by the works of August Strindberg, the writer with the largest and most colorful vocabulary in the history of Swedish literature.

One less fortunate consequence of Strindberg's stylistic talent has been his reputation as "master of the gibe," a literary epithet that reflects the misconception, long nourished both inside and outside Sweden, of Strindberg as an infuriated lunatic splurting uncontrolled, venomous diatribes on mankind in general and women in particular. Although much has been written in the last fifteen to twenty years to rectify Strindberg's mental and literary image, the portrait of him as a "bedeviled viking" and the assumption that his work lacks a disciplined form have lingered on. Recently an astute critic like Robert Brustein, referring to the usual Strindberg-Ibsen dichotomy in studies of modern drama, falls into the traditional trap when he states that "Strindberg lacks even Ibsen's grudging respect for external reality. . . . In his personal life . . . ego-worship often takes the form of severe psychotic delusions in which Strindberg loses his grip on reality altogether; and it robs his art of such Ibsenite virtues as self-discipline, detachment, and dialectical power." [1]

But Strindberg was by no means unaware of the problem of discipline, or, in literary terms, form. In fact, his writing represents not only the passionate output of a tortured mind but a conscious effort to find a structure capable of giving coherence to all the fragments he felt made up a human life, a problem that hardly faced Ibsen who remained much more rooted in nineteenth-century rationalism with its concept of the basic unity of the self. Strindberg, on the other hand, came close to being what Leslie Fiedler has recently called a *mutant* —a social pariah full of the ambiguity of sex, an outsider who transformed his basically erotic and disharmonic view of life into a *mythos* derived from eclectic metaphysical probings and from a gradual embracing rather than a harnessing of the irrational in the human psyche.

In studying Strindberg's early letters, some of them written during his late childhood and adolescence, one soon notices a certain restlessness of spirit and a rebelliousness of temperament that expresses itself both in school and family life. Born in 1849 as the fourth child (of eleven) to a steamship commissioner who had become a *déclassé* by his marriage to a former waitress and housekeeper, Johan August Strindberg grew up in a traditional patriarchal milieu filled with a stern, pietistic atmosphere that had detrimental effects on his impressionable nature. Between the taciturn father and the excitable boy there seems to have been little contact; the father showed some favoritism toward the eldest son in the family, Oscar, whose more stolid nature fitted better into the bourgeois pattern of the day. Johan August's achievements, on the other hand, appear to have been somewhat downrated; at one time his father allegedly dismissed him with the remark: "Well, Johan August is so strange! That one will never amount to much."

In his nervous sensitivity Johan August turned to his mother for affection and attention. There are indications that he never freed himself from what seems to have been an Oedipal attachment to her, with ensuing sub-conscious feelings of sexual guilt. His jealous guarding of the mother, his hatred of his father, and his anger at the latter's rather quick remarriage after Johan August's mother died when he was thirteen, read like reactions out of a psychology casebook. Throughout his entire life Strindberg was to be haunted by the vision of the perfect mother, profaned and hence turning destructive when becoming a sexual mate.

Strindberg's own account of his childhood and youth cannot always be trusted, for he liked to dramatize himself. By and large, however, he seems to have failed to play the role expected of him, and fears of softness, of effeminacy, continued to torture him long after he had reached adulthood. Many of his extreme reactions can be seen as attempts at compensating for doubts about his virility: his "Nietzscheanism," his admiration for military manners and scientific achievements, his attacks on women, and his occasional denunciation of literature (a woman's field). From time to time he projected his sexual ambivalence onto the social scene; he longed for the glory of the autocratic upper classes "as to a home-land," yet "his mother's slave blood" rebelled against his identification with them.

According to Strindberg's own account (*The Son of a Servant*) it was relatively early in the spring of 1867 that he became fully aware of the contradictions and tensions within himself, which culminated in his questioning of his personality as something fixed and permanent:

> When is one true to oneself and when false? And where is the self—which is supposed to constitute one's character? Here and there and every place at once. One's ego is not a unit in itself; it is a conglomeration of reflexes, a complex of urges, drives, instincts, alternately suppressed and unleashed.

Feeling that his self lacked a strong focus, Strindberg used to refer to himself as an impressionable person (*intrycksmänniska*), who in his search for identity became susceptible to a whole spectrum of ideas and cultural trends. The resultant eclecticism of thought never ossified into a fixed belief; absorption and questioning of a philosophical or literary approach often went hand in hand. Among the first to be attracted to Zola's Naturalistic dictum, Strindberg was also among the first to criticize it. Converted to a religious point of view in the 1890s, he soon afterward began to embrace a syncretist approach to religion, which allowed him maximum flexibility within a metaphysical framework and prevented him from becoming a strict dogmatist. Throughout his life, then, Strindberg's personality remained fragmented, evolving, chameleonlike, arrested only momentarily in its attempts at self-definition. But, like Pirandello half a century later, Strindberg was able to put into dramatic theory and form his insight into the fluidity of the human psyche. The first most striking example occurs in his discussion of the modern soul syndrome in the preface to *Miss Julie* (1888):

> Since the persons in my play are modern characters, living in a transitional era more hurried and hysterical

than the previous one at least, I have depicted them as more unstable, as torn and divided, a mixture of the old and the new. . . .

My souls—or characters—are patchworks of various stages of culture, past and present, pasted together from books and newspaper clippings, pieced up from scraps of human lives, patched up from old rags that once were fancy dresses—hodge-podges just like the human soul.

After a crucial psychic experience in the mid-nineties (the Inferno period) Strindberg's concept of the fragmented self resulted in the dramatic technique that was later given the name "expressionism," where the point of departure is the experiencing self, projecting aspects of its personality onto the stage in the form of split, dreamlike characters. In *A Dreamplay* (1901) Strindberg again preceded his work with a note in which he abstracts his personal experiences into a literary-psychological concept.

In this present Dreamplay I have sought to imitate the incoherent but ostensibly logical form of our dreams. Anything can happen; everything is possible and probable. Working with some insignificant real events as a background the imagination spins out its threads of thoughts and weaves them into new patterns—a mixture of memories, experiences, spontaneous ideas, impossibilities and improbabilities.

The characters split, double, multiply, dissolve, condense, float apart, coalesce.

The dream structure described in his foreword to *A Dreamplay* permitted Strindberg to discard the old structural pattern of causal interrelation between character, incident, and action. The fragmented self of *Miss Julie* now became a multifaceted personality revealing itself in numerous roles; in characters moving in and out of kinetic visions, all with the purpose to expose the inner feeling of a metaphysical condition.

Long before his Inferno period Strindberg had begun complaining about his inability to distinguish between dream and reality. In a famous letter to Axel Lundegård he wrote, after the completion of *The Father* (1887):

> I feel like a somnambulist. My life and my fictions are becoming one. I don't know whether *The Father* is a work of the imagination or whether my life is. . . . Through an excess of imagination my reality has become shadowy. I no longer walk the ground but float in an atmosphere not of air but of darkness.

After the Inferno period Strindberg was able to build this feeling of unreality into his new *Weltanschauung*: not only *his* life but all of life was a dream or a nightmare. This metaphysical vision enabled him to accept the irrational in himself without fear of insanity—that fear which he had sensed and dramatized in *The Father* —and without having to project it onto the female of the species. Thus Strindberg now began to see the source of painful living, not in womankind only nor in his personal destiny but in the immutable conditions of existence. The dream-play form grew out of this broadening of Strindberg's philosophical and psychological basis and can, in fact, be seen as an objectifying process analagous to but not identical with the process that led up to the writing of the preface to *Miss Julie*.

After he finished *The Father*, a play permeated with a tone of subjective agony, Strindberg wrote *Miss Julie*, a drama that moves in a socially definable reality. His first work for the stage after his Inferno crisis was *To Damascus*, an autobiographical drama that maintains the same tension between external reality and a hallucinating mind as *The Father*. A few years later when he began work on *A Dreamplay* he was reminded of certain technical aspects of the *Damascus* trilogy; now, however—as the tone of both the foreword and the *Dreamplay* itself brings out—Strindberg was detached from his subject matter ("but above them all stands the consciousness of the dreamer"). Like *Miss Julie, A Dreamplay* might therefore be considered an important, controlled effort to convey, without the intrusion of the author's private self, Strindberg's approach to life and art. In the pre-Inferno play he accepted a milieu defined by social hierarchies as his objective correlative; in the post-Inferno work he tried to recreate the universal and autonomous world of our dreams. In one play he assumed the role of analytical scientist; in the other the part of divine *Stellvertreter,* of omniscient dreamer. In both cases the attempt was made to subsume the suffering artist to his structured art.

About the time Strindberg completed *A Dreamplay* he began to resume, in his diaries and novellas, an old discussion from the 1880s of the artist's objective role. More and more he stressed his acceptance of himself as a creative, yet anonymous self. He now reserved his greatest admiration for Goethe (the classicist, not the romantic). When bearing in mind that this was the kind of writer he wanted to emulate, it seems indeed ironic that Strindberg should have gone down in literary history as an author who never transcended his own self-absorption but made his art his private expression. A quotation from an essay by Strindberg entitled "The Poet's Children," written toward the end of his life, reveals the discrepancy between the most prevalent critical view of him and his own conception of himself as an artist.

You are a writer and must effect reincarnations already here; you have the right to invent pseudonyms, and at every stage speak his language whom you impersonate; you have to make homunculi, you have to practice autogamy . . . The writer should have no grave and his ashes should be strewn before the wind, and he should live only through his works, if they possess vitality.

In view of Strindberg's claim to personal anonymity, it seems a further mockery of fate that upon his death he was buried with such ceremonious tributes that he himself would have frowned upon the whole affair. His accolades were found, however, not among the by and large conservative literary critics of his time but in groups of young socialists and radicals. This was both ironic and fitting. Certainly, Strindberg often felt drawn to the plights of the lower classes. Yet, in his private life he displayed the pedantic traits of a traditional household patriarch and he tended to identify the good life with a world of bourgeois values. In his perpetual quest for an emotional foothold, Strindberg's existence took on a set pattern with repeated returns to the middle-class fold. There he found the things he apparently needed: a daily routine with fixed hours and set meals; the company of a woman fulfilling her role as mother and homemaker rather than sexual and intellectual companion; a social atmosphere without any economic pressures.

Though an advocate of domesticity, Strindberg nevertheless married three professional women who could hardly fulfill his desire for roosting bliss. And not only did his rebellious temperament help undermine his financial security, but his dichotomous nature disclosed itself in a constant urge to destroy what would seem to be the very foundation of his existence. In his intellectual work he was fully conscious of his great literary talent, yet distrusted it to the point where he abandoned the world of imagination and launched himself as a Faustian alchemist and gold-maker. Identifying with the romantic role of the outcast, Strindberg nevertheless found himself unable to accept the consequences of his defiance: social isolation fed not only his pride but also his paranoia.

Strindberg's Janus-nature also expressed itself on the religious plane, in his movement between blasphemy and subjection, between a concept of God as a punishing Jehovah and a forgiving Father. In his philosophical explorations his ambivalence led him to be equally attracted to the intellectual aristocracy of Nietzsche and the natural democratic thought of Rousseau. In his approach to women it left him a passive worshipper *and* an aggressive misogynist. Thus contradictions seem to be inherent in all areas of his life and no doubt account for the fact that *tension* is the keyword of all his activities and the basic element in his literary output.

2

Master Olof: A Political and Dramatic Firebrand

On the surface it would seem that Strindberg drifted into literature. A precarious economy and a sense of rootlessness led him to try a number of occupations before he discovered one day that he could use his experiences creatively. Having graduated from the gymnasium in the spring of 1867, Strindberg spent the following summer as a tutor and went to the University of Uppsala in the fall to study humanities. His studies never led to a degree and he soon left the university to become a substitute teacher. A few months later he decided to study medicine but changed his mind; instead his thoughts turned to the world of the theater. He prepared to become an actor but failed; depressed, he took opium and spent a few days in semicoma. Awakening again to reality he felt a fever take hold of him and, according to his autobiography, he now began writing a play, which he finished in four days. Carl Reinhold Smedmark has shown, however, that these events were somewhat rearranged by Strindberg; apparently he wrote his first play before rather than after his opiate crisis.[1] In any event he was encouraged by friends and by an instructor at the theater to continue to write and subsequently produced a contemporary drama, *The Free-thinker,* and a tragedy based on a classical motif, *Hermione.* In 1871 he completed *The Outlaw,* a drama set in Iceland; it was performed without much success but led to a stipend from the King of Sweden, which enabled Strindberg to return to the university. His second stay in Uppsala was, however, as rebellious as his first and he soon left the city. He now decided to become a journalist and a professional writer. In the following summer (1872) he finished his first important work, the historical drama *Master Olof*.

The action of *Master Olof* takes place in sixteenth-century Sweden, during the reign of Gustav Vasa. Luther's attacks upon papistic rule reverberate in Swedish society; his disciple Olaus Petri (Master Olof) helps free the Church of Sweden from Rome's domination, not realizing at first that he is the King's convenient tool: Gustav Vasa needs money and advocates the reformation in order to secure the State an income by confiscating the land and property of the Church.

As a contrast to Olof, who is young, impressionable, and unsure of himself, Strindberg introduces Gert, the Bookprinter, an anarchist who is not satisfied with a religious reform but insists on a political revolution. Gert joins forces with the anabaptists in planning a murder of the King. Olof is drawn into the plot, but when imprisoned with the revolutionaries and condemned to death, he retracts. The play ends as Olof sinks down in shame on the stool of repentance while Gert, who faces death defiantly, pronounces his verdict of "renegade" over him.

Before writing *Master Olof*, Strindberg's absorbing mind had received impulses from many literary sources: Ibsen's *Brand*, Goethe's *Götz von Berlichingen*, Schiller's *The Robbers*, and Shakespeare's histories. Partly under this influence Strindberg decided to break with the conventional history drama in Sweden, and instead of writing a play in verse, adhering to the three unities, he created a prose drama with a loose form and multiple scene changes.

In his first draft of *Master Olof*, Strindberg's overruling feeling was one of idealistic pathos, inspired by a Kierkegaardian sense of calling. In Scandinavian literature, Kierkegaard's existentialist demand had found its embodiment in Ibsen's drama *Brand*, the story about an uncompromising parson who sacrifices his family and himself for his beliefs. The early Master Olof was in many ways a kin to Ibsen's fanatic churchman. But Strindberg came to read Georg Brandes's work, *The Emigrant Literature*, which questioned the value of Kierkegaard's abstract and ascetic idealism. Brandes criticized Ibsen's Brand, "whose moral, if it were realized, would force half of mankind to starve to death from love of the ideal."

Under Brandes's influence, and possibly also as a concession to historical truth, Strindberg changed the outcome of his play and let Master Olof compromise with his youthful ideals. Olof, at first depicted as a revolutionary who shunned no obstacles to win his goal, now became a vacillating reformer, a passionate youth tossed about by the manipulating actions of others. This emotional instability of the Master Olof figure eventually undermined his potential as a moral leader. That role was instead taken over by Gert, the Bookprinter and fanatic visionary. In the early draft Gert was merely an intriguer, a traditional dramatic type; now he became a political revolutionary, whose actions were dictated by principles rather than private ambitions.

Strindberg's final conception and handling of Gert is such that *Master Olof* has been called "grotesquely unhistorical." [2] Although Strindberg knew how to recreate a milieu that seems historically accurate, he took the same liberties as Shakespeare in telescoping time and space or arranging groups of people. Much impressed by Georg Brandes's essay on Hotspur, which stressed Shakespeare's use of minutiae, Strindberg proceeded to introduce incidental but realistic details. From

Shakespeare he also took the method of juxtaposing tragic scenes with comic interludes: the tavern scenes in *Master Olof* are directly patterned upon Falstaff's drinking bouts in *Henry IV*.

In spite of its many literary sources, *Master Olof* is a remarkable work for a twenty-three-year-old playwright who had, as yet, only a limited knowledge of the stage and hardly any native tradition to fall back upon. A comparison between Strindberg's first major play and the dramatic works of his contemporaries reveals at once that in Strindberg Swedish drama had received its first modern practitioner.

But those who formed Sweden's literary establishment and also controlled the native theater were not about to accept Strindberg into their fold. *Master Olof* became in fact the first target in a lifelong battle which Strindberg fought with an older generation of Swedish writers. The play was particularly susceptible to criticism because Strindberg had adapted a popular dramatic genre—the historical play—to entirely new moral, psychological, and theatrical principles. To depict Gustav Vasa on the stage was not unusual; but to present this king, who had gone down in Swedish history as a popular rebel against Danish tyranny and an idealistic reformer of the church, as an expedient manipulator and an exponent of cynical Realpolitik was indeed shocking. And to transform Master Olof, the great Lutheran churchman, from a burning revolutionary to a vacillating renegade was unpardonable. When these factors were coupled with the robust prose language of the play and its deliberate flaunting of traditional dramatic rules, *Master Olof* aroused in Sweden's literary and theatrical sectors the furious outcry of *blasphemy*.

That Strindberg was still uncertain of himself as a writer and dramatist is borne out by the fact that during the period between his completion of the prose version of *Master Olof* and his breakthrough as a novelist with *The Red Room* in 1879, Strindberg revised his play a number of times. During the entire 1870s he made several futile attempts to get his different versions of the play produced. (The prose version was finally performed in 1881, the so-called verse edition of 1876 was staged in 1890.)

In the course of his many revisions, Strindberg lost a good deal of faith in the individual's capacity to determine the course of history. Gradually he also gave up Shakespeare as his model; he cut the realistic tavern scenes and simplified the characters in order to obtain a more clearcut drama of ideas. As a result of Strindberg's giving in to his own doubts and to traditional stage demands, we get in the end a play full of striking poetic language but one in which very little is left of the dynamic personal conflicts that characterized the original prose version of *Master Olof*.

3

From *The Red Room* to *On the Seaboard*
Fiction 1879–1890

While at work on the first version of *Master Olof* Strindberg was employed as a journalist in a Stockholm newspaper. Although recognized as a talented reporter, he
offended the editor with his bold language, and after an
argument he left his job. For the next two years he
supported himself as a freelancer until he published, in
the fall of 1874, an article about the Royal Library; the
result was an eight-year employment as a member of its
staff.

Two crucial events occurred in Strindberg's life in the
seventies: he joined a coterie of young artists who met
regularly in the so-called Red Room at Berns' Restaurant
in Stockholm, where they discussed current literary,
philosophical, and political questions; and he made the
acquaintance of Siri von Essen, a young married baron-
ess and would-be actress, who was to become his first
wife at the end of 1877.

After a stormy courtship, which ended in Siri's divorce
from Baron Wrangel, Strindberg settled down to a quiet
and relatively idyllic home life. This was a productive
period in his life. Despite the failure of *Master Olof* he
continued to write, mostly articles and essays, but also
a collection of short stories based on his impressions of
student life in Uppsala, *Från Fjärdingen och Svartbäcken*
(translated as *Town and Gown*). After his marriage he

left the bohemian group at Berns, and, once having this time of his life at some distance, he began writing the novel entitled *The Red Room.*

The plot of *The Red Room* revolves around the idealistic and inexperienced journalist and would-be poet Arvid Falk who is exposed to various aspects of Swedish life in the late 1860s. As he becomes aware of the unscrupulous behavior of people in all walks of life, he is disillusioned and depressed to the point of suicide but is rescued from self-destruction by Borg, a medical acquaintance, and in the end reconciles himself to life. He gives up—at least temporarily—his attempts to reform society, withdraws from the group of bohemians with whom he has associated, gets married, and finds himself a hobby as a student of numismatics. Thus between the two extreme aspects of life that he has encountered—the world of economic upstarts and swindlers, of ambitious fops and hypocrites, and the world of bohemians, potential revolutionaries, and advocates of a philosophy of indifferentism—Falk creates a niche for himself in the secure milieu of esoteric scholarship.

The Red Room was conceived somewhat in the same spirit as the novels of Zola and the brothers Goncourt, that is, Strindberg adopted the role of scientific examiner of man and his environment. Strindberg later denied any knowledge of Zola at the time of his conception of *The Red Room,* but he was well aware of the Naturalistic credo, which had reached Scandinavia through Georg Brandes, whose exhortation to contemporary writers to adopt the viewpoint of social analysts and to set problems under debate had not gone unheard. It is likely that Strindberg had the current Naturalistic demand for factual correlatives in mind when he chose to call *The Red Room* not a novel (i.e., a work of free fabulation) but "sketches from the world of artists and writers." The contemporary temper of the book is also revealed in Strindberg's critique of the artist as a creator of beauty.

The two most important characters in *The Red Room*, Arvid Falk and his more naïve but also more radical companion Olof Montanus, a sculptor, have in common their failure as reformers but also share a growing awareness of the futility of art. Arvid Falk publishes a volume of poetry, which is well received in both the conservative and the leftist press. One day, however, he happens to read a review in the paper *The Incorruptible*, which claims Falk's poetry to be "neither worse nor better than that of his contemporaries, but just as selfish and insignificant."

But Falk's full recognition of the uselessness of his poetry occurs only after he has listened to Olle Montanus's chaotic attempt to puncture contemporary Swedish chauvinism. It is after this fiasco that Olle Montanus commits suicide by drowning, leaving behind him a few notes and aphorisms, in which he also criticizes the role of the artist: "the much talked-of artistic instinct . . . rests on a broad base of longing for freedom, freedom from useful work; for this reason a German philosopher has defined beauty as the non-useful."

Although the late 1870s were a time of growing social and political unrest in Sweden—the first strike of any importance took place in the city of Sundsvall in 1879 —the literary climate was still ultraconservative. In the fall of 1879 the Swedish Academy of Arts and Sciences elected two new members, Carl Nyblom, professor in aesthetics, and Carl David af Wirsén, established poet and critic. Both now pronounced their poetic creeds. Nyblom stated that the poet's task was "to give, in the light of ideals and in the form of beauty, a solution to the riddles that arise from the depth of the human heart." Af Wirsén declared that the goddess of poetry was "of heavenly origin and adds a holy content to the entertainment she offers." [1] It was precisely this general artistic norm that Strindberg rejected in *The Red Room*; one understands why his realistic study, with its blunt, disillusioned rendering of contemporary life and its refusal to maintain the image of the artist as an upholder of ideals and a creator of beauty, came as a shock to Sweden's literary establishment.

Strindberg's ambition in writing *The Red Room* was not only to present a scathing picture of Swedish society and destroy the Neoplatonic myth of the artist; he also wanted to create a philosophical novel about a sensitive young man's initiation into life. Recent criticism has stressed the connection between *The Red Room* and the nineteenth-century *Bildungsroman*. Arvid Falk has thus been compared to the prototype in the genre, Goethe's Wilhelm Meister. Both heroes are "vaguely defined but surrounded by carefully differentiated mentor figures." Both represent man as *l'homme naturel*. [2]

Arvid Falk is beyond doubt a Strindbergian *intrycksmänniska*, insecure about himself, easily influenced by others. He is in other words an excellent model for a hero in an educational novel. He combines curiosity and receptivity, guilelessness and sensitivity; he is a *tabula rasa* that makes him both an experiencing self and a sounding-board for others.

This dual function of Arvid Falk as both subject and object is reflected in the juxtaposition of two styles in the novel, one lyrical, the other critical and bitter. If one reads the lyrical passages only, one might imagine *The Red Room* to be a sentimental mood novel, while the sections that contain philosophical conversations or presentations of public institutions mark the work as a social satire. But it is Strindberg's continued interest in the central character that holds the disparate parts of the novel together. [3]

In the first half of the book the approach to society is that of caricature—the influence from Dickens has been noticed here.[4] But as Arvid Falk's knowledge of public life increases and Strindberg's rancor deepens, grotesque humor gives way to bitter philosophizing. In this disillusioned view of man as a social being, *The Red Room* joins company with *Master Olof*. The unscrupulous realist Gustav Vasa, symbol of earthly power, is here embodied in a whole series of figures, most of whom are identified by their social roles: Struve, the journalist who adapts himself to the political situation; Nicolaus Falk, the older brother and businessman, whose vision of life is limited to that of the stock market; Borg, the medical doctor who never neglects to seek personal recognition for his scientific findings and whose associations with Falk seem dictated by curiosity rather than compassion or sympathy.

When confronted with these men who govern society, Arvid Falk, the idealist who turns renegade, cuts a pitiful figure. He is a subdued Master Olof, continuously guilt-ridden, a politically aggressive but soft-hearted fellow who is most often described with such adjectives as meek, timid, submissive. He has been compared to Rudin and Nesjdanov, the sensitive and somewhat decadent idealists in Turgenyev's works, for instance *Fathers and Sons*, much read in Europe at the time.[5] Although Falk does not end up in their complete atrophy, he certainly embodies a good deal of the *fin-de-siècle* hero in European literature.

Arvid Falk survives his initiation into corrupt society but his recovery is told us indirectly, by Borg in a letter to his friend Sellin. To many readers Borg's summary letter has seemed like a hasty postscript from the author and a compositional *faux pas*. Yet it is possible to see the ending of *The Red Room* as part of a psychological pattern which Strindberg sets up at the very beginning of the novel and pursues with rhythmic persistence throughout the work. This pattern is related to Arvid Falk's manic-depressive personality, his oscillation between aggressive vitality and morbid despondency.

In the much-praised opening scene of the book ("Stockholm in Bird's Eye View") Arvid Falk stands on a hill overlooking the capital. Strindberg juxtaposes his hero and the city he sees, so that the two moods of Stockholm, conveyed by the busy activities of the harbor and the nostalgic ringing of church bells, correspond to the dualism in Arvid Falk's personality: he is a man of his times, a potential political activist, but he is also a romantic idealist, a passive dreamer. As he regards the city below him, he is filled with energy, but he also feels as if he were facing an enemy: "his nostrils widened, his eyes were flaming and he lifted his fist as if he wanted to challenge the poor city or threaten it." In the same moment, however, the church bells start ringing, and Arvid Falk turns away from the view of the bustling city; listening to the bells his face becomes soft; he feels alone but at peace with the world.

A similar movement from a confrontation with reality to escape and recovery through communion with nature characterizes Arvid Falk's behavior throughout the book. However, in a few posthumous notes his friend Olle Montanus reveals to him that peace through pastoral living is as great a self-deception as the creation of art: "I . . . fled into nature where I lived in meditation, which made me infinitely happy—but this happiness seemed to me a selfish pleasure, as great, yes even greater, than the pleasure I felt during my artistic work."

After Montanus's death Strindberg's task is to find for Falk an alternative to Olle's suicide. Without irony one might perhaps call Arvid Falk's decision to marry an analogy to Olle Montanus's exploration of the unknown. In Borg's final letter we meet again the aggressive Falk. Love has restored his health, as nature had done earlier. But although his engagement and scholarship are an escape from the social atmosphere of the Red Room, Falk does not withdraw completely from other people. The one important difference between Falk's new situation and his earlier attempts at recuperation is that love has enabled him to confront other persons successfully: in wooing the young girl, he has challenged his prospective father-in-law and has won his respect. One notices also that Falk's future wife is a schoolteacher and thus embodies a new, useful type of woman, as opposed to the female parasites that Arvid Falk has encountered earlier in the novel—Mrs. Nicolaus Falk who sponges on her husband, and Agnes Rundgren, the actress who lives like a prostitute. Falk's growing self-trust at the end seems no *volte-face* albeit Strindberg treats it in a somewhat cursory manner.

The Red Room was received with mixed feelings by contemporary critics but it fared well with the reading public, stabilized Strindberg's economy, and made him a well-known writer almost overnight. Stimulated by the success, Strindberg continued to produce copiously. No small part of his publications in the following years was made up of scientific and cultural treatises and articles; his subjects ranged from a study of the language and history of China—he knew Chinese and had already behind him a certain experience as a translator—to a thesis on Swedish hard liquor before 1772. But his major work was a two-volume survey of the cultural history of Sweden.

In writing this work, Strindberg was inspired by the same democratic pathos and radical view of society which had dictated parts of the satire in *The Red Room.* His ambition was to present a new approach to history. Instead of concentrating on kings, generals, and other

leading military and political figures, he aimed at show-
ing that the history of a country was the history of its
people.

Side by side with his ability to infuse dramatic life
into his historical characters, Strindberg had a strong
desire to prove the rightness of his convictions. All his
life he retained a reverence for documentary material,
and he shared the respect of his time for the scientist,
the man of facts and objective analysis. But in the long
run Strindberg had neither the patience nor the complete detachment from his material that could make
him a reliable scholar. His Swedish history proved to
contain factual errors and bold suppositions that laid
it open to criticism, especially among the traditional
historians of the day who agreed with Strindberg's
authoritative predecessor Erik Gustav Geijer that "the
history of Sweden is the history of its Kings." Strindberg, out of an insatiable need to answer his critics,
made a poor show of his defense, which probably contributed to the general neglect of the merits of his work
(i.e., Strindberg's presentation of an immense, often
hitherto unknown material and his ability to depict and
telescope the past in colorful and dramatic tableaux).

Strindberg was not satisfied with answering his critics
directly but burned with a desire to prove wrong all
conservative and bureaucratic elements in society. Out
of his indignation at the negative reception of his *Swedish History*, he published an attack on the men and
women in power, entitled *The New Kingdom* (1882),
a satirical pamphlet more cutting in its social criticism
than *The Red Room*.

The public reaction to *The New Kingdom* was immediate and fierce. Conservative critics saw it primarily
as an act of mudslinging, while more radical reviewers
regretted that the book seemed more an attack on
specific individuals than a rebellious social document.

Latter-day critics have been able, however, to appreciate the book's biting portrayal of contemporary humbug. But when Strindberg left Sweden with his family a year after the appearance of *The New Kingdom,* he had few supporters in either the traditional or the modern camp. The following reaction to Strindberg's departure from Sweden was by no means unusual:

> Mr. August Strindberg will shortly leave Sweden to settle abroad, the reason being, according to rumor, a state of mental aberration. In any case, one cannot but congratulate him on such a wise decision, which would seem to be caused by the most biting necessity. All that Mr. Strindberg can now strive for is to make himself forgotten as soon as possible . . . Mr. Strindberg's latest effort in writing books will no doubt mark the last station on his road downhill.[6]

Before his going abroad, first to Paris and later to Switzerland, Strindberg had also completed a series of short stories with a historical setting, a kind of fictional companion-piece to his *Swedish History,* which he called *Swedish Fates and Adventures.* In some ten tales he presented in fictional form various aspects of Swedish life from the Middle Ages to the nineteenth century. Originally he had intended to call his work "The Chronicle of the People," for the emphasis lay on life among the lower classes. Yet the collection offers a cross section of Swedish society in the past. It contains tales about noblemen and monks, artists and farmers, merchants and artisans. Often Strindberg creates dramatic tension by confronting the representative of one social group with that of another. In the first tale, entitled "Cultivated Fruit" (translated as "Over-Refinement") a nobleman, Sten Ulvfot, is thrown face to face with plebeians. In "Evolution" monks resist in vain the members of the King's force. In "Peter and

Paul" the tension arises from a clash between a farmer and a merchant.

The milieu-painting in these stories seems authentic enough, but the tales are nevertheless anachronistic in spirit. In many of them Strindberg appears as a disciple of Rousseau dressed in historical garb. A dominant theme is his criticism of urban life, which is depicted as brutal and parasitical and before which both overly sophisticated men like Sten Ulvfot and sturdy farmers like Peter have to succumb. City living is also associated with man-made authority; its laws are capricious and often unjust.

The negative reception of *The New Kingdom* was probably the catalyst that drove Strindberg to leave Sweden. But an examination of the early tales in *Swedish Fates*—a second volume was published many years later—shows that they contain, in spite of their straightforward picture of reality, an escapist element which is so persistent it seems to reveal an anchoring in the author's personal life. Sten Ulvfot commits suicide by drowning. Kristian in "Unwelcome" sails to a foreign country. Peter hints at the possibility of self-annihilation.

That Strindberg had long contemplated leaving Sweden is corroborated by a letter to Edward Brandes, dated June 1881, in which he wrote: "When I have finished my history of Swedish culture, which will unmask the entire Swedish nation, I shall go into exile to Geneva or Paris and become a writer in earnest!" But Strindberg's exile was not only based on a personal disenchantment with the Swedish way of life. It was very much in the spirit of the times. A number of more or less prominent writers and painters from all the Scandinavian countries resided then in central or southern Europe: Ibsen, Björnson, Jonas Lie, and Georg Brandes, to mention a few.

Strindberg arrived with his family in Switzerland in the fall of 1883; his stay abroad was originally planned for a year but came to last nearly six years, during which time his family resided in some twenty different places. The period was a crucial one for Strindberg; he now produced and published over twenty books—short stories, poetry, dramas, essays, novels. His marriage oscillated between moments of idyllic happiness and growing suspicions about his wife's fidelity. During the 1880s Strindberg also got to know several leading Scandinavian writers and through Georg Brandes he came in contact with Friedrich Nietzsche whose ideas intensified his increasing misogyny and pushed him further away from his earlier democratic view on social matters.

It was not really until after 1884 that Strindberg's stay abroad took on the aspect of an escape from Sweden. What changed his life from voluntary exile to paranoic flight was the legal repercussions and public reaction to a collection of short stories—*Married*—which he published in September 1884. *Married* was aimed at being a reply to Ibsen's and Björnson's "feminist" views as expressed in A *Doll's House* and A *Glove.* Strindberg's concept of marriage was at this time both modern and conventional. He opposed an intellectual approach to "the woman question," a fact that made him seem conservative to many; but his attitude was, on the other hand, much too sensual to please those who subscribed to the traditional role of married women. Strindberg's reaction against the marriage of convenience and his advocacy of less stilted (although not lax) relationships between young men and women aroused the public opinion. Yet the suit brought against *Married* concerned blasphemy rather than supposedly immoral sexual allusions. The trial centered around the following passage from the story entitled "The Reward of Virtue" (trans. as "Asra"):

His confirmation took place that spring. The moving scene in which the lower classes promise an oath never to interfere with those things which the upper classes consider their privilege, made a lasting impression on him. It didn't trouble him that the minister offered him wine bought from the wine-merchant Högstedt at sixty-five öre the pint, and wafers from Lettström, the baker, at one crown a pound, as the flesh and blood of the great agitator Jesus of Nazareth, who was done to death nineteen hundred years ago. He didn't think about it, for one didn't think in those days, one had emotions.

Although he was not convicted of the charges brought against him but, on the contrary, was celebrated as a popular hero, Strindberg could not free himself from the idea that the trial had been instigated by feminists, among them the Queen herself. His economy suffered as a result of the trial, which in turn intensified his bitterness. In the following year, when he published a second volume of *Married*, he presented an entirely different picture of the relationship between man and woman. Even though the first two stories in the collection retain something of the idyllic tone of *Married I*, the others reveal that Strindberg had now left behind him his Rousseau-inspired, genial, and optimistic view of male-female relations and had moved closer to Nietzsche's woman-hatred, which eventually was to culminate in a concept of woman as an intellectually inferior but morally unscrupulous being, a scheming bloodsucker and vampire. Married life was seen as a form of mental and emotional extortion; and woman, by nature a parasite, had the upper hand. The preface to *Married II* closed with a pathetic warning: "Look out, Men!"

The *Married* trial had convinced Strindberg that he should really pursue a scientific rather than literary career. He began publishing a number of articles on

nonliterary subjects, as well as a cultural study and
travel book entitled *Among French Peasants*. It was in
this same scientific-oriented spirit that he set out, in
1886, to write his autobiography. Still retaining his contempt for works of pure fiction, which he considered
primitive, effeminate, and distorting, Strindberg claimed
that a writer should be a social reporter, a documentary
analyst. The one document which he could use as an
authority was his own life. Strindberg now believed that
every human being could be an author and he suggested,
half in earnest, that every citizen send his autobiography
to the communal archives.

It has often been assumed that the major part of
Strindberg's literary production was autobiographical
and that he used literature as a means of restoring his
mental balance. But although his work might appear to
lend itself to the Freudian thesis of art as a form of
sublimation of personal psychic problems, Strindberg
does not always employ a symbolic language where the
psychologists have taught us to expect one; while in
other instances he puts on a mask when our moral
taboos would not call for one. He can reveal himself
shamelessly but he can also disguise reality. To him it
was no contradiction to write apropos of *The Son of a
Servant*: "Much is arranged . . . but I have tried to be
honest."

As a result, *The Son of a Servant* is a difficult work to
pinpoint. It is neither a straightforward autobiography
nor a formal novel, but a hybrid of the two. It may seem
at times a self-study in the tradition of St. Augustine's
and Rousseau's *Confessions*. Passages of moral self-
probing succeed sections of histrionic self-exposure. But
The Son of a Servant also contains philosophical parts
in the tradition of Goethe's autobiographical writing.
It is a work obviously aimed at telling the story of Johan
August Strindberg; but it is told in the third person, as

if the author wanted to achieve some distance between his private self and the personal material upon which the book is based.

Strindberg was only thirty-seven when he, having settled in Switzerland, began to write *The Son of a Servant*, and several major events in his life and the bulk of his literary production lay ahead of him. The book is written in four parts, of which the first ends in 1867, when Strindberg passed his student examination and left home. The second part, entitled "Period of Fomenting" tells of his youth, his time as a student at the University of Uppsala, and his various occupations up to the year 1872. Part 3, subtitled "In the Red Room," depicts him as a journalist and poet and ends with his meeting with Siri von Essen–Wrangel. The fourth part, finally, covers the decade 1877 to 1886, but was not published until after his death. The years 1875–77, during which time Strindberg wooed Siri von Essen and prepared for his marriage, are not included in *The Son of a Servant*. Strindberg had planned to insert them in the form of letters exchanged between him and his future wife. But this correspondence, called *He and She*, was not published until the first edition of Strindberg's *Collected Works* began to appear in 1919.

Strindberg's memory of the past is often colored by his present attitude of intellectual aristocrat. The book tells us actually as much about Strindberg as he was in 1886–87 as it depicts him when he was a young man. His analysis of his own earlier works should, for instance, be studied with caution, for he often reads into them conceptions and ideas that are of a much later date than the works themselves.

Strindberg's antifeminism, which is most noticeable in the first part of *The Son of a Servant*, tends to color his portraits of his parents. His father becomes a martyr, "the provider for all, the enemy of all"; his mother takes on certain aspects of bourgeois decadence: "She drank coffee in bed in the mornings, and she had two nurses, two servants and Grandmother to help her. In all probability she did not overexert herself." On the whole Strindberg regarded the family collective with violent hatred at this time, which resulted in his famous diatribe on marriage:

> Splendid, moral institution! Sacred family! Divinely appointed and unassailable establishment where future citizens are to be educated in truth and virtue! The supposed home of all the virtues, where innocent children are tortured into their first falsehood, where wills are broken by tyranny, and self-respect killed by jostling egos. The Family! Home of all social evils, a charitable institution for indolent women, a prison workshop for family breadwinners, and a hell for children!

With such attacks Strindberg followed in the tracks of Rousseau, whose confessions were meant to be an object lesson on the flaws in current education and family upbringing. In Strindberg's work as well as in that of his French predecessor we meet a self-conscious man commenting upon his childhood, and not a boy absorbing life in the unconscious manner of children. And like Rousseau, Strindberg was tempted to concentrate on the gloomy aspects of his childhood; his key words are those that form the title of the first chapter —frightened and hungry.

In depicting his childhood, Strindberg pays more attention to psychological than physiological details, but his overruling approach to his own background is one of social class-consciousness. Here the title of his autobiography has something essential to tell: in his own opinion Strindberg was a social outcast, the son of a servant. It was a view of himself that he was to retain,

off and on, until the end of his life. Ishmael, the biblical
son of Abraham and his servant Hagar, whom jealous
Sara drove into the desert, became his spiritual kin, as he
had been to many Romantic poets, although Strindberg
did not seem to have been aware of the Ishmael parallel
directly until the end of his life, when he sat down to
write the play *The Great Highway*.

Strindberg's momentary adoption of an aristocratic
philosophy coincided with the writing of the second
half of *The Son of a Servant* and led him to modify his
social position. He now places Johan in an ambivalent
middle position on the social ladder and sees repercussions of this in the boy's generally vacillating attitude,
in his religious questioning which still contains enough
of his childhood faith to make it impossible for him to
become a convinced atheist, and in his approach to art,
where he regards him as both a romantic and a naturalist, "like the garter snake which still has the lizard's
rudimentary feet under its skin."

That Johan stands in the center of *The Son of a
Servant* is beyond dispute. His self-absorption is at times
enormous, his constant need to assert himself leads him
often to adopt Gulliver's perspective among the Lillipu-
tians. Yet Johan is never oblivious to the people around
him, and he realizes his dependence upon them; he
knows that man is a social being who develops through
contact with others: "The personality does not develop
out of itself, but out of every soul it comes in touch
with it sucks a drop, like the bee collecting its honey
out of millions of receptacles but re-melting it and passing it off as its own."

Thus despite his preoccupation with himself, Johan
does not emerge as a hermit-artist. He is hypersensitive
to the point of being neurotic—and yet extraverted. A
large portion of *The Son of a Servant* deals with his
reaction and response to his family, to his teachers, his

friends, the whole of society. Strindberg is a master in telescoping political, religious, and moral trends in Sweden, and his language has a force and a speed that inevitably draws the reader into the sphere of life that he depicts. To read *The Son of a Servant* is not only to read "the evolutionary history of a Human Being"; it is to stand face to face with a whole era in Swedish life.

A *Madman's Defense* (1888), originally written in French under the title *Plaidoyer d'un Fou*, may be regarded as an appendix to *The Son of a Servant*, although it is more bitter in tone and more detached in its approach to the subject matter. Axel, a would-be writer, falls in love with Maria, a young married woman of the aristocracy. After a passionate courtship, Maria obtains a divorce and marries Axel. The rest of the book tells of the disintegration of Axel's and Maria's marriage, centering around Axel's disillusionment, endless fears, and suspicions that Maria has been unfaithful to him. The situation is resolved at the end but has driven Axel to the verge of madness.

Until recently it has been customary to approach A *Madman's Defense* as Strindberg's protest against Siri von Essen's presumed charges of mental illness. In Maria, Strindberg exposed Siri to the public and hoped thereby to prove his own sanity and prevent his wife from getting him committed to an asylum. In all likelihood Strindberg's marriage furnished the raw material for A *Madman's Defense*. Yet, as Rinman and Johannesson have shown,[7] much of the subtlety and psychological irony of the book is lost if one reduces it to an attack on Strindberg's first wife.

The first part of A *Madman's Defense*, depicting Axel's courtship of Maria, is somewhat set off from the rest of the book. It is largely told in the past tense and takes on an aura of memoir. Maria, seen through Axel's eyes, is a distant figure in an intriguing, largely outer-oriented novel that ends in the union of the two lovers.

The rest of the novel is mostly told in the present tense and resembles inner monologues depicting a situation that is still valid. Maria becomes more of an elemental force and less of an individual; she is, in fact, at times abstracted into almost grotesque proportions. Axel's suspicions of her unfaithfulness fill him with exasperation but also with pity, which forces him to forgive her: "And the more I suffer from my maenad's perversions, the more I make an effort to glorify her madonna head."

Axel's search for the truth about Maria turns *Defense* into a nightmarish plaidoyer. Axel is caught in the vicious circle of the neurotic person whose problematic nature and unresolved conflicts lead him into the same situation over and over again. The essence of *A Madman's Defense* is not so much the welling forth of a husband's unjust accusations against his wife as a series of emotional fluctuations which together give us the picture of a man spellbound by jealous passion, possessed by his own search, haunted by his suspicions. Axel is as much victim as prosecutor, and during his struggle to resolve the conflict he only succeeds in giving Maria a number of acceptable reasons for suspecting him of being mad, reasons which he is compelled to misconstrue. But by seeing Axel in the double perspective of culprit and dupe, Strindberg leads the reader into a world of amorous and hateful duelling where it is irrelevant who is at fault or who is victorious. What matters is the interminable search for a guilt that may or may not exist. Axel senses that the search constantly backfires: "The bond that binds me is not a chain of iron that I could break off, it is a cable of rubber that stretches itself. The harder it is stretched, the more violently it pulls me back to my point of departure."

Axel seems to be endowed with a good deal of Strindberg's subjective fury. Yet, *A Madman's Defense* has also an element of detachment similar to the third-person perspective in *The Son of a Servant.* Axel's and Maria's love affair and marriage is delineated with observant clarity, but also conveys a mood of impassioned frustration—as if told by someone watching his own execution in a nightmare.

To evaluate *A Madman's Defense* as Strindberg's attempt to write a whitebook of his marriage to Siri von Essen is to reduce it to a judicial document and to ignore its relevance to modern psychological fiction. Kafka knew better. According to Max Brod, he read for a long time nothing but Strindberg's autobiographical works and, we may surmise, it was not out of any gossip interest in Strindberg's private life but because he recognized in a book like *A Madman's Defense* a foretelling of his own novels and of such characters as Joseph K., the haunted and frustrated pursuer.

Before completing *A Madman's Defense,* Strindberg had written a novel which he later referred to as "an intermezzo scherzando between the battles"—*The Natives of Hemsö.* Many critics in the past have expressed surprise at the fact that in the midst of a private crisis and while living in a foreign milieu, Strindberg was able, in the novel *The Natives of Hemsö,* to depict with great objectivity and faithfulness life and nature on an island in the Stockholm archipelago, among people whose customs and thoughts differed very much from his own. But if we are willing to recognize Strindberg as a writer who was as observant of social milieus as he was hypersensitive to people with whom he was emotionally involved, and who was constantly looking for ways of transcending or analogizing his personal experiences, *The Natives of Hemsö* becomes no anomaly in his production but rather the rural counterpart of *The Red Room,* more burlesque in tone but no less satirical in its approach. Like the earlier novel, *The Natives of Hemsö* was conceived long after Strindberg had withdrawn from the actual setting of the work, the island of Kymmendö in the Stockholm archipelago.

The novel tells the story of Carlsson, an enterprising but not very persevering landlubber who arrives at Mrs. Flod's run-down farm on the island of Hemsö. Through scheming and an ability at organizing (including bringing paying summer guests to Hemsö from the city), Carlsson wins the confidence of Mrs. Flod and marries her, much to the resentment of Gusten, Mrs. Flod's son from an earlier marriage. Carlsson persuades Mrs. Flod to change her will in his favor, but after discovering Carlsson in an amorous tête-à-tête with the maid, Mrs. Flod makes Gusten destroy the will. While out searching and spying on her husband, Mrs. Flod has been taken ill; she dies just before Christmas and her body is taken to the mainland for burial. But the ice floes at sea are severe and the boat capsizes, with Mrs. Flod's coffin falling overboard. Carlsson drowns while Gusten manages to reach safety.

The Natives of Hemsö begins with Carlsson's famous and much-quoted arrival: "He came like a blizzard on an April evening." From the start it is this farmhand picaro who stands in the center of the book. It is through him primarily that we get to know Hemsö. But he does not always represent the author's point of view; he is too much involved in the action to function merely as an outsider and observer, and he is drawn with as much irony as the natives on Hemsö.

The action in *The Natives of Hemsö* spans a period of three years. Strindberg concentrates, however, on the first two summers and the third winter, telescoping the rest of the time into a few pages. That the summer season dominates the story is hardly surprising since Strindberg had little experience and knowledge of the archipelago in the winter. But the seasonal outline is also in keeping with the symbolic movement of the novel, which revolves around three events—the feast of haymaking; the wedding of Carlsson and Mrs. Flod; and the death of the two central characters.

The Natives of Hemsö is not, however, a tautly composed novel. Conflicts and tensions that have no relevance to the seasonal and symbolic progression of the book are numerous. Rudiments of Strindberg's earlier antagonism toward city life can easily be found and are interwoven with another of his favorite motifs, the battle between the upper classes and the unsophisticated upstart.

With the arrival of the city guests to Hemsö, Carlsson's position is solidified. But his greatest triumph is his brief participation, during the third summer, in the guild of city entrepreneurs. Having sold an islet to a stone quarry company, Carlsson is invited to the inaugural dinner, which releases his megalomania.

> When he got back home Carlsson swelled with bliss; he offered *punsch* to everyone, including those in the kitchen; he showed the stock certificates which looked like gigantic government banknotes. . . . He had grandiloquent plans; he wanted to found one big consolidated firm for all the salted herring in the skerries, bring coopers from England and charter freighters of salt directly from Spain.

Soon afterward the enterprise collapses and Carlsson loses four thousand Swedish crowns. But with his "seabird nature," he shakes off the unpleasant feelings and has soon regained his self-confidence. Such sudden changes in attitude are part of Carlsson's psychological makeup. But they may also be seen as an in-

dication of Strindberg's own rather episodic handling
of the novel. Its characters live by their quick movements and impulsive, often irrational reactions; its landscape emerges in swift, although often detailed tableaux. Here, too, a mood is not sustained for long, but
pastoral scenes alternate with naturalistic catalogs of all
living things on and around the island.

Although Strindberg could often ridicule the naturalist's photographic approach to his subject matter, he retained a fondness for scientific jargon and a weakness for
factual material. A few months before beginning *The
Natives of Hemsö* he wrote to his editor, Albert Bonnier: "It nauseates me to be only an artist. My intel-
ligence has developed from imagining [*fantiserande*]
to intellectual thinking [*tänkande*]." Yet, in *The Natives of Hemsö* the artist dominates over the man of
science. The factual terminology plays a subordinate
role and the total impression is visual, as testified by
the famous portrait artist of the time, Richard Bergh:

> Strindberg saw things in the same way as we painters
> do. . . . In his writing he never for a moment forgot
> the surroundings, the landscape. . . . He never saw
> people and events in isolation. He saw them as parts
> of a whole, saw them against a given background, in a
> given light, in a given moment of the day and the year
> —just as painters see them.[8]

But what discloses above all Strindberg's imaginative
approach to his subject matter is his abundant use of
metaphor. It has rightly been claimed that Strindberg
is the most image-creating writer that Sweden has ever
had.[9] Usually, his metaphorical language draws upon
the urban milieu in which he grew up, and upon science
and technology. In *The Natives of Hemsö*, however,
nature furnishes much of the metaphorical material
and is used in such a way as to fuse with the narrative

and psychological content of the novel. And taken as a whole, the metaphorical abundance, together with the swift rhythm of the language, accounts for the fact that although its dramatic content is weak and its psychology often shallow, *The Natives of Hemsö* is a very dynamic story.

A year later Strindberg produced another work of fiction set in the Stockholm archipelago, *Skärkarlsliv* (*Life in the Skerries*), a collection of short stories which contains the important novella *The Romantic Sexton on Rånö*. This novella is of great interest as a prelude to Strindberg's post-Inferno production. It is one of his earliest refutations of the Naturalistic approach to life in fiction. In writing the novella, Strindberg expressed fear that it would not appeal to the general public "who only wants absolute copying without using the author's brain as a stereoscope, but without which the perspective cannot be achieved."

The plot concerns Alrik Lundstedt, a fisherman's son, who goes to Stockholm to study music. An imaginative young man, he begins to embellish reality and dreams of being engaged to a beautiful young girl. He has to give up his ambitions of becoming a composer and ends up as an organist in the skerries. Here he eventually loses his ability to re-create a world of illusions; his childhood memories plague him and he goes to confession in order to reveal an old crime he has witnessed. In the end he marries the lighthouse keeper's daughter, and instead of dwelling in a dream world, he plays with his children who are "real toys."

Strindberg's conclusion is a compromise and probably echoes his own tension between the world of imagination and the world of everyday reality. Lundstedt's bourgeois marriage is regarded by Strindberg as a kind of recovery (one is reminded here of the development of Falk in *The Red Room*). In letting Lundstedt re-

linquish his daydreams, it is as if Strindberg already sur-
mised and tried to ward off his crisis in the mid-nineties when imaginative and real phenomena began to
merge for him.

After completing *The Romantic Sexton on Rånö*
Strindberg wrote a preface to *Life in the Skerries*. The
organist is now dismissed as a victim of subjective fantasies resulting from his isolation at sea. As if to prove
the shortcomings of the imaginative personality,
Strindberg, putting on a moralizing tone, compiles a
great deal of geological and biological jargon. In this
respect, as well as in the negative view of isolation, the
preface to *Life in the Skerries* anticipates the novel *On
the Seaboard*, published in 1890, which tells the story
of Axel Borg, an inspector of fisheries, who arrives on
an island outside of Stockholm. Borg is an intellectual,
hypersensitive individual who considers himself superior
to his environment. A brief love affair fails and Borg is
abandoned by the young woman. The natives regard
him with skepticism and hostility. His isolation intensifies his feelings of being not only unique but also persecuted and finally leads to his suicide.

Plotwise, *On the Seaboard* has a certain similarity to
The Natives of Hemsö. But as Walter Berendson has
shown,[10] theme, style, and tone are different in *On the
Seaboard*. Axel Borg is conceived as a much more conscious and articulate man than the rather naïve
Carlsson, and he is drawn without irony. The presentation of the native population has also undergone a
marked change. The comic but fairly sympathetic portrayal of the natives of Hemsö has now turned into a
bitter picture of "a half-starving, useless stock of people." The statement is Borg's rather than his author's,
but Strindberg's sympathy for the inspector remains
strong, though not complete, throughout the novel.
Numerous letters from this time also reveal his fearful

attraction to an intellectual aristocracy such as Axel Borg represents.

The crucial philosophical source behind *On the Seaboard* is Nietzsche's idea of the superman which Strindberg had also used in the artistically weak novella *Tschandala*, published a year earlier (1888). Strindberg, having read Nietzsche in the spring of 1888, was immediately attracted to his extreme individualism. Later the two writers exchanged dedicated copies of their recent works (Nietzsche his *Götzendämmerung*, Strindberg his drama *The Father*) and responded with mutual admiration. But toward the end of 1888, Nietzsche's megalomania reached abnormal proportions, and Strindberg received word that the German philosopher had been sent to an asylum. Recognizing in Nietzsche a spiritual kin, Strindberg was now haunted by a fear of sharing his fate.

For a time Strindberg subscribed to Nietzsche's violently antireligious views. Hence he made his hero in *On the Seaboard* a scientist for whom self-reliance is a primary virtue and who excels in blasphemous denunciations of the Christian faith, attacking its emphasis on meekness and submission to one's destiny. Yet Strindberg infused an element of decadence in Axel Borg, thus making him a kin of the *fin-de-siècle* heroes of European literature. That Borg meets defeat among his inferiors is also in keeping with Strindberg's personal conviction; to him the intellectually superior individual was always persecuted and hated by the pariahs in society, whose strength lay in their unscrupulous methods and lack of moral conscience. Likewise, Strindberg thought of nature, or the strong and primitive forces in life, as a superior enemy to the sensitive and sophisticated person: Axel Borg fails in his attempt to use his scientific learning to control nature.

The language in *On the Seaboard* seems to contain in

itself a tension between disciplined learning and unrestrained barbaric vitality. Strindberg's colorful and exuberant depiction of scenery and milieu attains at times the same forceful immediacy and imaginative power as in *The Natives of Hemsö*; but coupled with such passages we find a factual style so meticulous in its botanical, zoological, and geological details as to appear precious. Although this style may be in keeping with Borg's learned approach to nature, it reaches at times the proportions of parody.

On the Seaboard is an uneven and pathetic book. But as a prelude to the personal crisis that Strindberg went through in the mid-nineties, it is a revealing work. His conception of nature as a demonic power is present: Borg's tenacity in approaching his milieu scientifically attains the quality of a magic formula, a ritual to ward off evil forces. Occasionally, detailed descriptions of objects surrounding Borg move out of the strictly naturalistic sphere and prove that Strindberg already looked upon reality with the eyes of the symbolist. Images from *On the Seaboard* come back in Strindberg's post-Inferno drama *A Dreamplay*, and so does the concluding reverie of the dying Borg as he meets the ambivalent "All-mother, from whose bosom the first spark of life was lit, the inexhaustible fountain of fertility of love, the origin of life and the enemy of life."

4

Sexual Warfare on the Stage
From *Sir Bengt's Wife* to *The Dance of Death*

With the publication of *The Red Room*, Strindberg
had become known as the realistic standard-bearer in
Swedish literature. It was a position he could only accept halfheartedly, for in sentiment if not in thought
he remained a romantic. The dramas he wrote in the
early 1880s, *The Secret of the Guild, Lucky Per's
Journey,* and *Sir Bengt's Wife,* reveal his ambivalence
before the new literary trend which he himself had
helped to realize in his novel of 1879. Strindberg's vacillating mood also leaves its marks—both attitudinal
and formal—on his famous so-called naturalistic
dramas of the 1880s: *The Father, Miss Julie,* and *The
Creditors.* It also leads, in 1901, to the creation of a
new type of domestic drama—*The Dance of Death*
—where realistic details are compressed to form a grotesque and nightmarish atmosphere that anticipates
certain plays within the absurdist theater.

The two major motivations behind the conception of
The Secret of the Guild seem to have been Strindberg's
promise to write suitable parts for Siri von Essen, and
the fate of *Master Olof,* which was rejected by the
Royal Dramatic Theatre in favor of a conventional
historical drama by Edward Bäckström. The action of
The Secret of the Guild (which Strindberg later claimed
inspired Ibsen to write *The Masterbuilder*) takes
place in fifteenth-century Uppsala and tells of two

41

rival architects who compete for the finishing bid on
the cathedral. The less competent but popular man
wins, while the other is reduced to a journeyman. But
justice is done as one of the church towers collapses
during a spring storm, thus revealing the ineptitude of
its builder.

Like *Master Olof, The Secret of the Guild* is an
ideological drama with a historical setting, but it also
contains a metaphysical dimension that points to a later
phase in Strindberg's dramatic production. The play is
built according to the theory of retribution that the
eighteenth-century Swedish biologist Linneus put forward in his so-called Nemesis philosophy,[1] which was
to be a crucial idea in certain of Strindberg's plays some
fifteen years later. However, *The Secret of the Guild*
lacks the personal vision of Strindberg's later dramas;
its action never seems the outcome of inexorable fate
and is not sustained by a pervasive belief in transcendental powers. Rather, the play remains a skillfully con-
structed and somewhat naïve demonstration of poetic
justice.

The second play from this time, *Lucky Per's Journey*,
is in some ways an inversion of *The Secret of the Guild*.
While the latter play maintains a realistic frame but
contains elements of superstition which we associate
with romantic literature, *Lucky Per's Journey* has the
romantic form of a fairy tale—it was inspired apparently by H. C. Andersen's stories—but develops into a
social satire, modeled upon the realistic novel *The Red
Room* and anticipating *The New Kingdom*. In a series
of kaleidoscopic scenes Strindberg lets his protagonist
come in touch with the most sought-after aspects of human existence: wealth, fame, power, and freedom from
social bonds. All prove to be disappointing, and the
play becomes a reckoning with a life devoted solely to
the pursuit of personal happiness. Only through hard

work and unselfish love can Per attain peace of mind.

Lucky Per's Journey is a fantasy pilgrimage. We travel with Per from episode to episode, as independent as the seemingly unconnected sequences of Strindberg's later dream plays. At each station Per is disillusioned but whisked away and given new hope by the magical Lisa, who is the one essential link in Per's travels and also an instrument for his redemption. If Per foreshadows such seekers as the Stranger in *To Damascus* and the Hunter in *The Great Highway*, Lisa anticipates Indra's daughter in *A Dreamplay*.

With his third play from the early 1880s, *Sir Bengt's Wife*, Strindberg returned once more to an earlier epoch in history, fifteenth-century Sweden. But again the historical costume was merely a cover-up for current ideas and attitudes on the part of the author. Strindberg's growing antifeminism and his beginning disillusionment at his first marriage helped create an ambivalent woman character. The young women in *The Secret of the Guild* and *Lucky Per's Journey* are romantic abstractions, representing a love of innocence that scorns sexual advances; they are embodiments of the eternal feminine in the tradition of Faust's Gretchen and Peer Gynt's Solveig. But Sir Bengt's Margit becomes the first in a long row of Strindbergian half-women—disharmonic creatures unable to accept the conventionally passive role of their sex but equally incapable of living at peace in an active masculine world. Lacking the intellectual equipment of the male sex but goaded by primitive desires to dominate, these modern half-women intrude upon the male domain. When successful they exist as parasites or vampires, feeding upon their more talented and intelligent husbands; when failures, they are either driven to self-destruction or else chastised and ridiculed.

Through his portrait of Margit, a half-degenerate

young lady of the nobility who refuses to accept her
traditionally wifely role but fails miserably when trying
to partake of the material problems around her, Strindberg meant to furnish an answer to Ibsen's *A Doll's
House*. But like all of Strindberg's contributions to the
feminist debate which raged in Scandinavia at the time,
his play is meaningless as a reply to Ibsen's drama.
Ibsen saw in Nora Helmer a human being stunted intellectually and morally by social customs and traditions. Strindberg, on the other hand, defined woman by
her biological function only and was convinced that
she represented a lower stage on the evolutionary scale
—at the peak of his antifeminism he claimed to have
proved that women had one more vertebra than men, a
rudiment of a tail which brought them closer to their
animal ancestors. Thus, according to Strindberg, in trying to get insight into the world of men, a modern
woman like Nora Helmer not only questioned the conventional concept of a woman's place in society but went
against the very laws of nature. With the term *half-
woman* Strindberg implied a woman with masculine
ambitions but also a monstrosity of a woman, a traitor to
her sex and one of nature's freaks.

All of the three plays discussed here seem
conventional when compared to Strindberg's later
dramas. They are filled with characters who are little
more than theatrical clichés; with unfortunate archa-
isms and a stilted nineteenth-century dialogue. Yet they
contain the nucleus of all the major elements in Strindberg's better known plays. *The Secret of the Guild* introduces the problem of suffering and guilt, which
was to be central to Strindberg in the mid-nineties and
on. *Lucky Per's Journey* foreshadows, by its picaresque
form, such dramas as *To Damascus* and *The Great
Highway*, and possesses scenes which in their bitter
absurdity and rancid criticism of social hypocrisy anti-

cipate the squabbles of the four faculties in A *Dream-play* and the Millers and Schoolmaster episodes in *The Great Highway*. And as the earliest of Strindberg's marriage dramas, *Sir Bengt's Wife* presents us with one of his most persistent themes: the incompatibility of the sexes and the possessiveness of love.

In 1886 Strindberg added another work to his anti-feminist collection, *Marauders* (later renamed *Comrades*). It is a mediocre play about a husband exploited by his untalented wife, whom he finally throws out of the house threatening to send her to prison if she dares return. The play soon degenerates into a prolonged, choleric, and petty argument and is constantly on the verge of becoming a parody of a serious domestic drama.

But in the following year Strindberg published his first marriage drama of importance, *The Father*, whose two major characters—a captain-scientist and his wife Laura—quarrel about the education of their daughter Berta. Through unscrupulous tactics, Laura gets the Captain to doubt his fatherhood and taunts him into a temperamental outburst. She gathers the support of the family doctor, and assisted by Margaret, an old nurse who under childish coaxing puts a straitjacket on the Captain, Laura brings her husband to the point of mental and physical collapse.

At the time of his writing *The Father* Strindberg had doubts about his wife's fidelity and his own fatherhood as well as suspicions of being the ridiculed model for Hjalmar Ekdal in Ibsen's *The Wild Duck*, the would-be inventor whose parenthood is put at stake. The essential factor behind Strindberg's conception of *The Father* (as well as *A Madman's Defense*, written a few months later) was not his household arguments with Siri von Essen or their alleged differences over the children's education, but the *uncertainty* as to whether he was living with a woman who was destined to destroy him or whether his lively imagination was helping to create a hell out of his life. His lack of definite proof, his feeling of unbearable suspense dictated his picture of marriage in *The Father*.

But although *The Father* has the violently subjective tone of an author's feelings welling forth suddenly and freely, it is not a straightforward, private confession so much as a man's projected vision of the irrevocable warfare of the male and female of the human species. When Strindberg sat down to write *The Father*, he saw himself as a typical representative of the modern male threatened by the arrival of matriarchy on earth. An article published in a French journal in 1886 by the sociologist Paul Lafargue had solidified his view. Lafargue claimed that the Greek drama, *The Oresteia*, reflected an epoch of violent struggles resulting in the destruction of a patriarchal society and the birth of a matriarchy. The author also suggested that similar struggles to reinstall a matriarchy were in the offing.

Strindberg interpreted matriarchy to mean a world in which women abandoned or abused their function as caring, motherly creatures and gave free reign to their unscrupulous, instinctively possessive psyches. In *The Father* he set out to depict, with great dramatic concentration, the process of such a woman who turns into a furious virago and kills her male prey through poisonous insinuations. The method that Laura uses—subconsciously rather than deliberately, according to Strindberg—to destroy the Captain was suggested to the playwright by his readings in popular psychology. A year before the appearance of *The Father*, Strindberg had published the essay entitled "On Psychic Murder," which was inspired by ideas put forth by the French psychologist Bernheim and the so-called school of Nancy, and which emphasized the use of hypnosis, suggesting the possibility of a person with strong will power to drive someone of a more sensitive mind to his death by undermining his self-confidence and gaining control over his actions.

In his essay Strindberg took as his point of departure a discussion of Ibsen's *Rosmersholm*. He regarded its female protagonist Rebekka West as a demonic schemer who sowed the seed of suspicion in Beate's (Rosmer's first wife) mind but was careful not to give her full proof of her husband's infidelity. Doubt and uncertainty brought Beate to her death.

Whatever one might think of such an interpretation of *Rosmersholm*, it is an interesting projection of the conflict that Strindberg dramatizes in *The Father*. His analysis of Rebekka West makes her very much a kin of Laura, and Rosmer's first wife is depicted suffering the agonies of the Captain in Strindberg's own drama. Unaware of her "instinctive vileness," Laura exerts her demonic power over her husband until he cries out: "You could hypnotize me when I was wide awake, so that I neither saw nor heard, but simply obeyed. You could give me a raw potato and make me think it was a peach." Like all psychic murders, Laura's cannot be proved since it leaves no visible clues behind.

The Captain accepts Laura's insinuations so readily as to make him cease to be convincing if judged by realistic standards. The temptation is strong to look upon him as a pathological character. But while some critics have pointed out the sick element in *The Father*—a relatively early student of Strindberg, Martin Lamm, referred to the play as "a hospital journal"—others have been reminded of the self-consuming emotions of Shakespearean drama. The hyperbolic, hysterical tone of the play and the lack of sensible reaction and verisimilitude in its male protagonist brings to mind a Timon, a Lear, or an Othello, just as the Captain's

paraphrase of Shylock's speech ("has not a man eyes")
seems a piece of well-placed borrowing.

Yet the Captain does not have the individual stamp
of a Shakespearean character. Strindberg's delineation
of his dramatis personae seems almost abstract. The
Captain, a man without a family name and a being referred to through his social position only, emerges as
a personification of the emasculated male. His military
standing functions symbolically only, as an indication
of his potential virility and serves primarily to put his
defeat and Laura's ruthlessness in sharper relief; it is a
man of physical stature and no weakling that is destroyed. The Captain's scientific preoccupations fulfill a
similar purpose in defining his intellectual superiority;
to Strindberg, a man's scientific perception was always
a weapon that could prove his basic sanity; once Laura
has cut the Captain off from his spectroscope analyses,
she has actually disarmed him.

The Captain, whom Strindberg conceived of as a
Nietzschean superman belonging to the same race of
men as Borg in *On the Seaboard*, is a creature of infinitely larger dimension than Laura or, for that matter,
any of the other characters in the play, male or female;
larger certainly than Nöjd, the trooper who unwittingly
launches the question of fatherhood in the first scene
and introduces the prevalent image of the female as a
seductive demon; larger too than the easily manipulated
doctor and the unctuous, henpecked pastor. The Captain's frustration and impotent rage attain further force
from the many allusions in the drama to mythological
figures of strength, victimized by deceitful women. He
is not fighting a nagging, small-town housewife and her
cohort of female supporters only; behind Laura loom
the ominous shadows of Omphale who curbed Hercu-
les, the epitome of male strength, by stealing his club,
and of Delilah, who rendered Samson defenseless by be-
traying the source of his physical power.

Laura is no more conceived as a realistic character than is the Captain. Her place in literature is not among the many lifelike portraits of middle-class women that have appeared in fiction and drama since Madame Bovary and Nora Helmer. The part she plays has little to do with that of an ordinary housewife—she is never seen carrying out any household tasks; when she discusses the budget with the Captain, it is only in order to set her will against his; and she never talks to those who help her run the ménage, except to old Margaret, the nurse, who is a bother to her until she becomes her accomplice. One need only compare Strindberg's presentation of Laura with Ibsen's depiction of Nora in *A Doll's House* to realize that the two women move in different orbits. The middle-class routine that defines Nora before her rebellion has no place in Laura's sphere of experience; her acts and her reactions are primarily designed to bring out her demonic features. Her passionate hatred overshadows almost completely her everyday duties and her marriage commitment, and it moves the action of the drama into a world of such heightened tension that it appears closer to a nightmare than to any tangible reality.

The Captain is in fact aware of fighting out a conflict that transcends the domestic domain, a conflict which is "like race-hatred," atavistic, lodged in the unconscious, and assuming the shape of "fantastic dreams." In that nightmare world dwells not only the destructive figure of woman as sexual mate but the pervasive spirit of the treacherous Mother. Even without a direct knowledge of Strindberg's oedipal love for his own mother and his resentment of his stepmother, one can feel emerging quite clearly in *The Father* his ambivalent attitude toward the maternal woman as both a giver and a withholder of love.

When the Captain moves before Laura like a massive giant of a child confessing his need to win her as a man,

Laura explains to him, "That was your mistake. The mother was your friend, you see, but the woman was your enemy. Sexual love is strife. And don't imagine I gave myself. I didn't give. I only took what I meant to take."

But even when reduced to a child, the Captain cannot be certain that the mother is his friend, any more than Berta, the daughter, can feel safe among the older women in the house. Berta's offstage grandmother, who exerts an ever-felt pressure on the household, fails to display any kind of maternal concern for her. Instead she takes on the character of an evil sorceress who tries to lure the granddaughter into the world of superstition which, according to Strindberg, has a particular fascination and relevance for the primitive female psyche.

Old Margaret, the nurse, has a slightly overbearing attitude toward the Captain, her former breast-child. Sharing with Laura a lack of moral insight into her actions—a feature which Strindberg felt characterized women, criminals, and animals—old Margaret can bring herself to put the straightjacket on the Captain after having reduced him to a docile child. Through her action old Margaret enlists in the long row of women who have betrayed the Captain throughout his life, so that he is finally convinced that all members of the female sex are his enemies.

The Father demonstrates that in the struggle between man and woman, between rational mind and primitive, self-absorbed will, the latter is victorious. The Captain, warrior, scientist, and family provider is defeated and destroyed. His intellect is broken, his atheism left unsupported even by the Doctor, the traditional rationalist in fiction and drama. The Doctor's final words that the stricken Captain might awaken to another reality are bitter when seen in the context of the play. For *The Father* is a drama in which

any reference to a spiritual extention of life carries
suggestions of female dominance, all the way from the
Pastor's role as henpecked husband rather than religious leader and Margaret's morbid intonation of a Bap-
tist hymn to the Captain's furious reference to "the
Goddess of strife" and his final "prayer" not to God but
to the Virgin Mary. The very ending of the play provides a final, ironic allusion to female omnipotence:
Laura and Berta, mother and child (the victor and her
token of power) embrace. The sexual threat, the challenge to dominance has now been removed. With the
Captain gone, Laura can resume her role as soothing,
protective, but all-powerful mother. The Pastor's
"Amen," which closes the drama, is really the cruel
blessing of the triumphant world of women.

Strindberg regarded *The Father* as a Naturalistic
play, and upon its publication he proudly sent a copy to
Zola, feeling that he had produced a drama in accordance with the tenets put forth in Zola's *Le naturalisme
au théâtre*. Superficially speaking, *The Father* does follow certain Naturalistic principles: it has a taut and
simple form; it ignores earlier demands for dramatic
exposition and blatantly dismisses a conventional in-
trigue; it provides an analytical key to its characters and
sees them in terms of hereditary and elemental forces
over which they have little or no control; it provides
verisimilitude in place, time, and action. Yet Zola's reaction to Strindberg's drama was rather tepid. He found
Strindberg's psychological delineation of the Captain
and Laura too superficial. He also hinted at Strindberg's
failure to present his dramatis personae and their problems in an objective, disengaged way. To Zola, the
biased fury of the play was a weakness.

It is possible that Zola's response to *The Father* challenged Strindberg to pursue his Naturalistic ambitions.
When he sent his next play, *Miss Julie,* to the editor in

August 1888, he proudly called it "the first Naturalistic tragedy in Swedish drama." [2] The play does seem much more of a premeditated and objective work than *The Father*.

It was part of Strindberg's Naturalistic ambition to construct a full-length play as a concentrated one-acter. In *Miss Julie* interludes like a mute midsummer eve's dance and a pantomime performed by the cook, Kristin, take the place of conventional intermissions. Furthermore, in his desire to maintain the illusion of a real drama taking place before the audience, Strindberg followed the Naturalistic demands for unity of time, place, and action. One also senses the impact of Naturalism in the story itself, which Strindberg was eager to emphasize as being "a case, a motif from life itself as I heard it spoken of a number of years ago, when the episode made a strong impression on me." [3] Finally, the playwright's desire to prove, with his drama, a law of nature—in this case the survival of the fittest—was in accordance with Zola's decrees.

The concentrated plot of Strindberg's drama concerns Miss Julie, a twenty-five-year-old woman of the nobility, who flirts with her father's valet, Jean, during a midsummer eve. After seducing Julie, Jean suggests that they flee to Switzerland in order to avoid a scandal at home but later changes his mind. Vacillating between despair and hope of escape, between disgust for and dependence on Jean, Julie finally chooses suicide, but only after Jean has exerted a hypnotic influence on her.

Jean, the opportunist who was once a laborer's son but has learned to live in the style of a gentleman, is, to quote from Strindberg's famous preface to the play, a "race-builder," a man of the future, representing "the new nerve-and-brain nobility," to whom Julie must succumb. It was Strindberg's belief that the evolution he depicted in *Miss Julie* was not only inevitable but also desirable. If it depressed anyone, said Strindberg in his preface, to see the downfall of a tragic figure, it was the spectator's own fault; instead of being sentimental about Julie he should realize that the time would come when "we shall be happy and relieved to see the national parks cleared of ancient rotting trees which have stood too long in the way of others equally entitled to a period of growth—as relieved as we are when an incurable invalid dies." A modern audience is not, however, likely to view the conflict between the hypersensitive Julie and the socially pretentious but brutal Jean with any great feelings of comfort. The reason for this is obvious: Strindberg's portrait of Julie in the play is much more sympathetic than his view of her in the preface.

The preface was written after the play, and its tone reveals a conscious attempt on Strindberg's part to disengage himself from his characters. The effort to transcend his private daemon, noticeable in the drama itself, was completed as Strindberg proceeded to view his dramatis personae as objectified products of his controlling artistic intellect. His cool analysis of Miss Julie as a creature of indeterminate sex is a case in point.

> Miss Julie is a modern character, not that the half-woman, the man-hater, has not existed always, but because now that she has been discovered she has stepped to the front and begun to make a noise. *The half-woman is a type* who thrusts herself forward, selling herself nowadays for power, decorations, distinctions, diplomas, as formerly for money. The type implies degeneration; it is not a good type and it does not endure; but it can unfortunately transmit its misery. (Italics mine.)

One might argue that because Strindberg felt compelled to develop *Miss Julie* within very limited bounds of time and place, its action is allowed to accelerate to a point where it becomes detrimental to the psychological plausibility of the drama. What Strindberg gives us in *Miss Julie* is a kind of dramatized synopsis of a relationship. Yet the concentrated swiftness with which he unravels the story of Jean and Julie has its fitting counterpart in the labile, hysterical mood of the title figure and in the brusqueness of Jean's character. It does not lead to a simplification of the dramatis personae; in that respect Strindberg remained true to his original intention of complicating the inner mechanism of the drama while simplifying its outer form. He departed from the classification in conventional drama of characters according to stereotypes, and in the spirit of French psychologist Ribot he attempted to dramatize a whole complex of human traits. As a result Jean is depicted as both servile and aggressive; Julie as both domineering and submissive.

The strength of the drama is psychological. Its social situation seems hardly relevant today, and if it is acceptable to us at all, it is because Strindberg works it into the subliminal texture of the play. The idea of social rising and falling compels Strindberg to include the exchange of dreams between Jean and Julie in the early half of the drama; Julie sees herself sitting on a high pillar, longing to fall down; Jean has a vision of lying under a high tree, wishing to climb to the top. Fortunately these dreams also function on a psychological level and reinforce the feeling that two incompatible people are driven together and that the catastrophe is almost a *fait accompli*.

Through Jean's seductions of her, Julie becomes a fallen woman, not only in the puritanical sense (which was relevant enough to Strindberg) but in a social-ethical sense as well; she loses her *noblesse oblige*, the trait that is the very foundation of life among the warrior nobility of which Julie is a relic. Julie is, in Strindberg's words, "the last of her race"; what becomes extinct with her is more than her personal family line; it is a way of life based on such concepts as pride, courage, and honor.

As a social upstart, Jean's conquest of Julie is a victory, the fulfillment of a childhood dream; as a small boy he watched Julie in a pink dress and white socks while he himself lay among the weeds and "wet dirt that stank to high heaven." Remembering Strindberg's common association of soil and manure with sexuality, Jean's memory refers not only to a dream of social egalitarianism but to a sexual fantasy as well. Now when Julie has been socially degraded and Jean has possessed her in body, the roles have been reversed; the valet sees his mistress as a flower turning to muck; and in a literal sense Julie, dressed sloppily and with a dirty face, looks as if she had been soiled and trampled on, whereas Jean retains his fastidious elegance, brushing off any speck as easily as he turns away Julie's pleadings.

Yet, the final scene of the play shifts once more the parts of the two lovers. For while Julie walks to her death holding her head high, Jean cringes in fear before the count's bell. The servant is victorious as a male, but he remains a servant. The aristocrat is defeated sexually and socially, but she dies nobly. In an early draft of the play Strindberg made this development even more clear by having Julie die on her own initative. Pulling the razor out of Jean's hand, she said scornfully: "You see, servant, you could not die." Even in the final version of the play Julie's suicide is to be regarded —as Strindberg suggests in his preface—as "the nobleman's *harakiri*, the Japanese law of inner conscience which compels him to cut his own stomach open at the insult of another."

Strindberg claims in the preface to *Miss Julie* that he has challenged the rhetorical style and stilted dialogue of older drama: "I have avoided the symmetrical, mathematical construction of French dialogue, and let people's minds work irregularly, as they do in real life where, during a conversation, no topic is drained to the dregs, and one mind finds in another a chance cog to engage in. So too the dialogue wanders, gathering in the opening scenes material which is later picked up, worked over, repeated, expounded and developed like the theme in a musical composition."

This statement, which brings to mind Chekhov's art, could actually serve as an accurate description of a dramatic technique found much later in Strindberg's production, in *A Dreamplay* and in his chamber plays. But when applied to *Miss Julie,* it becomes only a half-truth; in this drama Strindberg's dialogue is still quite conventional even though one can see attempts at an allusive speech pattern, especially in the scene following the seduction.

But the counterpoint technique of the later dramas is hardly developed yet in *Miss Julie.* Instead Strindberg relies rather heavily on a symbolic pattern reminiscent of Ibsen's dramas—he uses objects or situations as metaphors designed to foreshadow the dramatic conflict. In the opening scene, Kristin is busy preparing a brew for Diana, Miss Julie's purebred bitch who has been consorting with a bastard dog—an all too obvious parallel to Miss Julie's own fate later on in the play. The ending is anticipated in much the same way—Julie gives Jean her delicate cage bird and, without hesitation, he breaks its neck, thus revealing both his own unfeeling nature and the role he will play in Miss Julie's final fate.

Such a calculating technique is hardly convincing in the work of a dramatist who usually aims at a more instinctive layer of our psyche. In the final analysis the technical design of *Miss Julie* seems too well made and the play rather survives in spite of it; it lives not on its Naturalistic premises or Ibsenite technique but on its emotional tempo, as always a very essential part of Strindberg's dramatic talent.

We know that Strindberg had difficulty with the ending of *Miss Julie* and that he questioned Julie's previous explanatory revelation of her past. These are precisely the passages which are set up according to Strindberg's Naturalistic conception of the human psyche; hence we must assume that the playwright sensed the incompatibility of some aspects of the contemporary literary approach to character and his own personal feeling for dramatic efficacy. Even so, Strindberg persevered in his ambition to write a perfect Naturalistic drama. In *Creditors* (1888) he claimed to have driven "the new formula" to perfection. He did away with the symbolic machinery of *Miss Julie*; reduced the action to concern the theme of hypnotic influence, and confined his conflict to three scenes only, involving three characters of practically equal importance. One of them is Tekla, a divorced woman writer who is now remarried to a painter, Adolf. Tekla returns after a short trip to find that her former husband, Gustav, has paid a visit. During Tekla's absence Gustav, has almost convinced Adolf, who is unaware of Gustav's identity, that he is being destroyed by Tekla's usurping nature. Later, Gustav arranges a tête-à-tête with Tekla, whereupon Adolf, who listens behind a door, falls down dead. Tekla now embraces her dead husband with all the despair of a loving wife.

This melodramatic action is built up around a triangular pattern, the meetings of Gustav-Adolf, Adolf-Tekla, Tekla-Gustav. The setting is an impersonal room in a Swedish spa, a fitting milieu for a drama that is entirely a clash of wills, based on the special relationship of the three characters (the not uncommon constellation of man-woman-rival) but without any anchoring in a personally colored environment.

Although *Creditors* pursues the Naturalistic program as delineated in the preface to *Miss Julie*, its dramatic conception seems closer to *The Father*. In *Creditors*, Strindberg splits the sadomasochistic tendencies in his own nature—Gustav becomes the aggressor, Adolf the martyr. Tekla is—like Laura in *The Father*—the personification of vile womanhood or, according to Strindberg, a picture of "woman as a small and stupid and nasty creature, as man's appendix and encumbrance, to be crushed like a barbarian or thief." [4]

Adolf is already half "dead" when Gustav finds him, for Tekla has devoured his soul in order to feed her own. Gustav calls it cannibalism: "Savages eat their enemies so that they'll get their strength for themselves. She has eaten your soul, this woman, your courage, your knowledge." Adolf agrees by adding: "And my faith . . . I gave, I gave, I gave—until I had nothing left for myself."

Tekla's evil seems absolute, dictated by her female nature, and Adolf's and Gustav's behavior is conditioned by it; their thoughts and actions are motivated by jealousy and a desire for revenge. Having a largely passive nature, Adolf has never carried out any ugly intentions against his former rival, "the idiot." But Gustav excels in giving cruel blows, as when he without reason tells Adolf with hypocritical sympathy: "You know, my dear friend—it gives me great pain to say this—but you have the first symptoms of epilepsy." In his distraught state of mind, Adolf becomes an easy victim of Gustav's insinuations; only too late does he discover Gustav's strategy—"You pull me out of the hole where I've fallen through the ice, but as soon as I'm out, you hit me on the head and push me under again."

Gustav is depicted as a kind of superman, shaped by Max Nordau, Nietzsche, and contemporary psychiatry, a man without God and without feelings but with a magnetic power over people and a detectivelike ability to discover their weaknesses. While Tekla instinctively feeds on others, Gustav dissects them. He is the superb controlling mind; a creditor who demands justice but does not judge morally, who holds people responsible but not guilty; all in strict accordance with the deterministic law of nature that Strindberg meant to demonstrate in this atheistic play. Gustav is his own God— Adolf, using the conventional image of God during the Age of Reason, once refers to Gustav as "a watchmaker" —but he is not the ultimate cause of the collapse of Tekla's marriage and the death of Adolf; he sets the machinery in motion and brings forth the innate sexual warfare between man and woman, or what he himself once hints at as one of "the discords in life . . . that never can be resolved."

Strindberg's own statement that he had written a drama that was "humane, charming, with all three characters sympathetic"[5] seems strange, for *Creditors* is a cruel and cynical play. On the other hand, Strindberg's reference to *Creditors* as a tragicomedy is extremely significant in the light of later developments in modern drama where, in the works of Ionesco and the theater of cruelty, we find a similar deemphasis on individual characterization and *Einfühlung* and have instead a presentation of the dramatis personae engaged in a fierce battle of dialectics. Although Strindberg's play has the detailed surface pattern of a Naturalistic drama, it presents us with an action that lacks normative verisimilitude and motivation. The outcome is a stylized drama with an almost metaphysical dimension, a grotesque black comedy where much of the power lies in a steady flow of argument through imagery built on allusions to cannibalism, torture, and anatomical dissection. Tekla is described by Adolf as "an intestine that carries away my will" and a surgeon who "destroys my brain with her clumsy pincers." Gustav's words are said to cut into Adolf "like knives" while their effect is like "the lancing of boils." Adolf's fate is reminiscent of "a picture by some Italian master—of a torture—a saint whose intestines are being wound out on a winch." Gustav refers to his dissection of Tekla as the cutting apart of a human soul, "exposing its entrails on the table." In keeping with the destructive emphasis in the metaphorical design of *Creditors*, one of the few stage props used in the play is the knife with which Adolf threatens to kill his wife.

Strindberg hoped to get both *Miss Julie* and *Creditors* produced by the Théâtre Libre, an avant-garde theater started in 1887 by André Antoine, a clerk in the Paris gas works. But he had to wait until 1893 before Antoine ventured to stage *Miss Julie*, which according to the producer was "an enormous sensation." In the following year *The Father* and *Creditors* appeared at another Paris theater, and Strindberg had won international recognition.

Soon after Antoine started his Théâtre Libre, Strindberg, too, began to play with the idea of creating a theater of his own. He had actually had such a project in mind as early as 1876 but nothing had come of it. Now, twelve years later, when he discovered that no theater dared produce *Miss Julie* and *Creditors* his old plans began to take new form, and in the late fall of 1888 he started The Scandinavian Experimental Theatre in Copenhagen. Its manager was Siri von Essen, with whom Strindberg was temporarily reconciled.

Strindberg wrote three one-act plays for his theater. The production collapsed, however, after only two performances. He modeled his plays upon Antoine's repertory where amateurs performed short one-acters, called *quart d'heures*. Having no resources for an exclusive stage, Strindberg gave his plays a simple scenic form with few parts and stage props—a form which happened to adapt itself to his current Naturalistic striving toward simplicity and thematic concentration.

Pariah, written in six days early in 1889, was adapted from a short story by Swedish writer Ola Hanson. It is a piece of human vivisection in the style of *Creditors*. Nietzsche, Poe, and the Italian criminologist Lombroso left their impression on the play, designed as a battle between an intellectual man and a fawning but ruthless criminal who is unmasked with much the same psychological cunning as Poe used in his detective stories. The dialogue is swift and cutting, but a great deal of the theoretical material on which the play is based remains undigested.

Poe's influence is also noticeable in *Samum*, a play set in the Orient. It tells of the murder of a French lieutenant, committed under hypnosis by an Arab girl. *Samum* combines Strindberg's infatuation with hypnotic experiments and a setting popular in contemporary Scandinavian literature (cf. Ibsen's *Peer Gynt*, act 4). But the Arabian desert was a place Strindberg could only depict with set clichés; he fell back on an excessive and grotesque plot and thus failed to bring the drama beyond the level of clever theatricality.

In *The Stronger*, the third of his one-acters, Strindberg returned once more to his familiar theme, the battle of brains. The play presents a variation of the frequent Strindbergian image of the vampire, the bloodsucking personality that attaches itself to another human being and feeds upon the victim until it has been deprived of its strength and identity. In *The Stronger* Miss Y appears at first to be the aggressor who has robbed Mrs. X of her husband's love; but in the end it is Mrs. X who

emerges as the "stronger," for she has cleverly absorbed
Miss Y into her very being: in acquiring Miss Y's personality, Mrs. X has also regained her husband's affection.

In all its brevity *The Stronger* is a psychological tour
de force. The very form of the play reveals that Mrs.
X's pliable nature, which we associate with a passive
personality, is merely a smokescreen that hides the truth
from Miss Y and the audience. Throughout the play it
is Mrs. X who *moves* on the stage, who does all the
talking, who, in other words, is active and alive, while
Miss Y is reduced to a passive onlooker and listener.

After the fiasco of the Scandinavian Experimental
Theatre it took almost three years before Strindberg
wrote again for the stage. He moved from Denmark
and returned to Sweden after more than five years of
absence. At home he lived through the final, dramatic
phase of his divorce from Siri von Essen, culminating in
a libel suit brought against him by one of his wife's
friends. It was a period as unhappy as the time following the *Married* lawsuit in 1884.

By this time Strindberg had consciously begun to
part company with Naturalism, which he felt had de-
generated into "a mechanical working method ele-
vated to an art form." The statement appeared in an
essay he published in 1889, entitled "On Modern Drama and the Modern Theatre," in which he attacked "objectivity, loved by those who lack a subject,
by those without a temperament, by the soulless as they
ought to be called." Strindberg now distinguished
between "grand naturalism which enjoys the struggle
of the powers of nature" and "petty realism which includes everything, even the speck of dust on the camera
lens."

Philosophically, Strindberg began to move away from Nietzsche. The superman concept of the battle of brains which for a long time had nurtured his literary inspiration was losing its interest for him. His proclaimed atheism was shaking in its foundation, and the religiosity of his childhood showed signs of returning at the same rate as his loneliness increased and his intellectual defense mechanisms collapsed.

In the spring of 1891 Strindberg visited Runmarö, an island outside of Stockholm where he had earlier spent some time with his family. In a mood of melancholic nostalgia he began to plan a fairy play for children. The work, entitled *The Keys of Heaven*, was designed as a paraphrase of *Lucky Per's Journey*, but Strindberg, now disillusioned, was unable to hold on to the basically optimistic mood of the earlier play.

The Keys of Heaven tells of Saint Peter, who having lost the keys of heaven, comes to the Smith and asks him to make new ones. But the Smith can do nothing until he has seen the lock. Together with Saint Peter and a mysterious person called the Doctor or Doctor Anonymous he sets out to find the gate of heaven. But he finds neither lock nor heaven. Toward the end of his fruitless journey the Smith's children appear before him as in a vision and he realizes that they represent the only heaven he will ever find on earth.

Strindberg's ambition to write a happy play for children collided not only with his disharmonic view of life but also with his desire to attack recent literary and philosophical trends in Sweden. *The Keys of Heaven* moves between scenes of forced gaiety and venomous lovemaking; between sentimental nursery memories and flat, topical satire. It is certainly not a very suitable play for children. But its naïvely didactic tone, obviously adapted to a young audience, makes the play a rather tedious experience for adult spectators too, and its sensual and philosophical content is better expressed elsewhere in Strindberg's production.

The Keys of Heaven is interesting, however, in that its kaleidoscopic, pilgrimage design implies a complete break with the controlled and simple form of Strindberg's plays from the 1880s. In structure *The Keys of Heaven* anticipates the *Damascus* trilogy, written in 1898 and 1901, although it does not possess the trilogy's thematic coherence. And in spite of lacking the metaphysical perspective of his later dramas, *The Keys of Heaven* might be seen as an early sign of the direction that Strindberg's life and art was to take. In its emphasis on Christian suffering, the Smith's journey touches upon the sacrificial element that was to become crucial in the playwright's later *Weltanschauung*.

The rest of Strindberg's production in the early 1890s seems like echoes from his Naturalistic period. He wrote a full-length drama, *Debit and Credit*, which is his last and rather distasteful flirtation with Nietzscheanism, as well as a number of one-act plays—*The First Warning, Before Death,* and *Mother Love*—that range in mood from excessive self-pity or cynicism to erotic badinage but maintain the concentrated form of the works from the late 1880s. The surface motivation behind these one-acters was Strindberg's renewed hopes of founding a theater of his own. When compared to most other dramas in the Strindberg canon, they appear mere trifles.

In the fall of 1892 Strindberg completed *Playing with Fire*, one of his few comedies, and *The Bond*, a dramatization of his memories of the divorce proceedings between him and Siri von Essen. *Playing with Fire* is almost Chekhovian in setting; an idle, upper-class family spends a hot summer in aimless activity and conversation, and in the midst of their ennui great passions flare up. A young man who comes on a visit attracts the

mistress of the house. Her husband is willing to re-
nounce her, provided the young man will marry her.
Under such circumstances the visitor flees in panic.

In *The Bond*, the male protagonist decides not to
escape but to face the issue. Strindberg, using what he
had once claimed to be the most adequate form for a
Naturalistic drama, a court proceeding, designed the
play as both a legal and moral reckoning. A baron and
his wife fight in court over their only child, "the bond"
between them, and the drama develops as a heated
argument full of mutual accusations, set against the
court's interrogation of the couple. In the end both
parties lose the child, who is to be brought up by two
jurymen.

Legal procedure and world order were parallel concepts to Strindberg. *The Bond* is not meant as a case
study only; its verdict over the Baron and his wife is a
verdict over Man and Woman; Strindberg's couple is
fighting out the universal and fatal battle between the
sexes. As in *The Father*, Strindberg wipes out the question of individual guilt, but the accusing tone in the earlier play has now mellowed to compassion. "We are
both to be pitied," says the Baron, a statement that
will reverberate with sonorous repetition in Strindberg's plays after the turn of the century.

One of these dramas, *The Dance of Death*, is often
discussed together with the plays of the 1880s, for like
these it conveys to us a playwright motivated in his
work by an intense belief in the perennial warfare between the sexes.

In *The Dance of Death* the battle is fought between
Edgar, a captain in the artillery, and his wife Alice.
Married for nearly twenty-five years, the couple spend
their time alone playing cards or quarreling with each
other. Both nourish longtime disappointments; the
Captain has not been promoted as expected; Alice feels

that she has sacrificed a great artist's career when she married Edgar. Their existence has the stability of life reduced to burnt-out hope and apathy.

Then, into their home comes Alice's cousin Kurt and, immediately, the tension mounts. But the presence of Kurt, a quarantine master, also cleanses the air. It is as if he absorbed all the psychic disease and hate of the house. Finally he has to flee because "there are corpses under the floor and such hatred, it is difficult to breathe." But once Kurt is gone, the Captain and Alice seem to be at peace and they are able to joke and laugh together. Kurt's therapeutic role is, however, something that eludes the couple, who call him a humbug and a weakling.

The Dance of Death seems at first glance to indicate a return to Strindberg's Naturalistic dramas of the 1880s. The play has only three characters; it observes the unity of time, action, and place, and has the single-minded thematic purpose of *The Father* and *Creditors*. But as the mutual threats of Alice and the Captain accelerate to a point of taking on the quality of both chimera and metaphor, the two combatants become more and more closely related to some of the grotesque characters in Strindberg's later chamber plays. Like these they are once-removed from the temporal and spacial dimensions of conventional drama. It is therefore useless to ask whether such people as Alice and Edgar *really* exist—as useless as attempting to lead the plot and the characters back to an actual situation or to known people. The lives of Alice and the Captain have some remote reference to reality; they represent countless couples tied to each other by habit and smouldering passion, to whom a severing of bonds would be both socially and psychologically unacceptable. But they also move into a realm governed by the verisimilitude of fantasy; the macabre concentration and outlet of pent-up emotion suggests a nightmarish world in which, fortunately, most people only dwell in moments of acute crisis or in their dreams.

In his concentration on a couple's mutual need to torture each other to death, Strindberg stages his Swedenborgian view that hell is a condition of mind expressing itself as destructive will—a belief dramatized half a century later by Jean Paul Sartre in his play *No Exit* ("L'enfers, c'est les autres"). The infernal atmosphere is reinforced by the locale of the play, a fortress on an island. With its suggestion of a prison (outside, the saber of the guard glitters in the sunset), it has a much stronger symbolic quality than, for instance, the living room in *The Father* or the hotel room in *Creditors*. Unlike the earlier dramas, *Dance of Death* conveys a world of complete isolation. *Creditors* took place in a resort spot, and *The Father*, the play that has usually invited comparisons with *The Dance of Death*, contained a full household of people; furthermore, the struggle between husband and wife concerned the life of their daughter, who was present throughout the play. In *The Dance of Death* on the other hand, the last servant has left the couple, the small community on the island has withdrawn from them, and even their children have gone to live elsewhere; their absence is in fact indicative of the utterly sterile life led by Edgar and Alice, who sit capsuled in ennui and bitterness and have only their hatred, their mediocrity, and their antipathy for the rest of society in common.

The mood of the play extends to the decor as well. Whereas in the Naturalistic dramas most pieces of furniture were strictly utilitarian (for instance, the desk and the lamp in *The Father*, the sofa in *Creditors*), details in the couple's home in *The Dance of Death* are a reflection of their owners' emotional state: the piano looms like a diabolic instrument and is used as such by Alice; the naked walls of the room reflect the barrenness of the married couple's life together. And, most important of all, the realistically motivated but odd telegraph contraption (the phone has been cut off), relaying messages from the outside world, captures the essential mood of the play, a strange fusion of frustration, anguish, and absurdity that links *The Dance of Death* with the drama of Pinter and Albee.

Part two of *The Dance of Death*, written upon the request of Strindberg's German translator who felt that part one was too gloomy a play, presents a development of the redemptive theme, suggested by the presence of Kurt in the earlier drama but now embodied in the Captain, whose sadistic impulses are given a moral function.

The central relationship in part two is that between the Captain and Kurt. The former emerges as a pre-study of old man Hummel in *The Ghost Sonata*, sharing his ambiguity as vampire-torturer and benefactor-liberator, while Kurt displays the same saintlike nature as the Student in the chamber play. The Captain now absorbs the hatred of the house as Kurt did in the first part of *The Dance of Death*. But whereas Kurt left the scene, the Captain stays to the bitter end, finally swelling into an ugly monster but perhaps dying, as Valency suggests, "as a scapegoat, a pharmakos, supremely self-sacrificial." [6] The Captain's Christ-inspired last words support such an interpretation; taunted and harassed by Alice who boxes his ears and pulls his beard, Edgar dies muttering "Forgive them for they know not what they do." Yet his redemptive power is limited. Although a change seems to come over Alice who no longer laughs hysterically, the dance of death goes on in the next generation: a brief scene between the daughter Judith and her fiancé Allan contains the embryo of that ruthlessness which goaded the Captain and Alice to torture each other for decades.

In *The Dance of Death* (II) the presence of the children reduces rather than intensifies the quality of abstracted nightmare. For while the presentation of sexual warfare as a vicious, never-ending circle results in a drama that seems very modern in its contextual rather than linear development, the effectiveness of such a play structure depends to a large extent on the condensation of the drama to a kind of *reductio ad absurdum*. Stringberg critics have most often objected to the second part of *Dance of Death* on the grounds that it is a tautological play. The Captain's changing psychological role in the two parts would seem to refute such a charge. The crux appears to be, however, that his scapegoat destiny is too close a parallel to Kurt's in part one. One wishes that Strindberg had worked out a compression of the two plays.

5

The Inferno Experience

In the early eighteen-nineties a strong and successful reaction against Naturalism, or rather against its literal-minded aftermath referred to as "shoemaker realism," dominated the literary climate in Sweden. Strindberg felt, with some justification, that he had anticipated this reaction. His imagination had never been attracted to the petty photographic aspects of Naturalism but rather to its exploration of deterministic thought, its demand for psychological multiplicity and concrete milieu painting. As early as 1888 Strindberg had stated in a letter that "Zolaism in natural scenery and staging seems to have run its course." He had mentioned Paul Bourget and Guy de Maupassant as the new trailblazers. Shortly afterward he saw in Edgar Allan Poe a literary soul mate.

Basically Strindberg had, however, too pragmatic and moral an approach to art and too universally oriented a mind to be attracted to the aesthetic and nationalistic trends that set much of the tone in Swedish literature after 1890. When he, in addition, came to regard the advocates of the new literary program as his competitors in a struggle for leadership, his wounded vanity helped solidify his position as dated Naturalist and literary reactionary. Forcing himself to hold on to an approach to literature in which he no longer believed whole-heartedly and to an art form which his imagination had drained, Strindberg found himself in an artist's cul-de-sac. So used up were his creative resources that when he left Sweden for Germany (upon the recommendation of fellow writer Ola Hanson) in September 1892, his ambition was not to renew himself as a writer but to pursue scientific studies while seeking recognition in his adopted country for his earlier dramatic works.

He succeeded in arousing a certain interest among German theater producers for his plays, but his extraordinary ability to offend those who wanted to support him meant that he did not harvest much, financially, from his stay in Germany. At the same time his preoccupations with science, which could occasionally take on manic proportions, led to a complete fiasco. His most important scientific work, *Antibarbarus*, which appeared in Germany in 1894, was a curious mixture of Darwinian aftermaths and medieval alchemy. But its negative reception only stimulated Strindberg to new efforts, at least for the next few years. All in all he published during the first part of the 1890s some six hundred printed pages of scientific hypotheses and theories.

Strindberg's German stay became little more than an episode in his life, but it restored his spirits momentarily. He had left Sweden without a family and without any friends and supporters. Some twenty years earlier he had broken with bourgeois society and moved into bohemian circles in Stockholm. Now the pattern repeated itself. Settled in Berlin, Strindberg began to frequent a cafe which he gave the name "Zum schwarzen Frenkel" and where he met a gay, temperamental, and unconventional group of Scandinavian, Polish, and German artists. He seems to have been somewhat of a coffeehouse dandy; he dressed elegantly and was much sought after by women. It was now that he met the

Austrian journalist Frieda Uhl, twenty-three years his junior, whom he married in May 1893, after a brief courtship.

Strindberg married three times and was divorced from all of his wives. Yet one might say that he was a monogamist who married the same woman over and over again. At the time of the wedding, this woman was an abstraction: a maternal creature but not clinging, self-contained but not domineering, loving and passionate but not aggressive, artistic-minded but without creative talent. Of the three women upon whom Strindberg projected this ideal, two were actresses and one a journalist. Although professional women, they were no immediate threat to Strindberg the productive artist and intellectual, which was no doubt one reason why he was attracted to them.

But Strindberg also sought an evil wanton in every woman he got to know, someone to whom he could transfer his own guilt feelings and nausea about sex. Needless to say, none of his wives was able to adapt to his emotional ambivalence, and Strindberg himself never resolved his need to seek both agape and eros, Mary and Circe, in the same woman.

Strindberg only lived with Frieda Uhl until August 1894, although the marriage was not dissolved formally until 1897. He soon became irritated by Frieda's efforts to get him recognized as a writer. His disharmonic state of mind expressed itself again in a restless moving from place to place. During two visits to Frieda's family home, Strindberg met, however, a person who was to have a certain influence upon his psyche, his mother-in-law Maria Uhl who was a pious Catholic. His religious groping began to be noticeable and he wrote in a letter from Dornach in July 1894: "What destinies now are in store for me I do not know, but I feel the hand of Our Lord resting over me."

A month later Strindberg was back in Paris where he parted from his wife in the street and was not to see her again. Now followed the period which Strindberg later, with reference to Dante's *Divine Comedy*, called his Inferno and which was to last until 1896–97. What Strindberg went through during these years was, as Gunnar Brandell has shown, not a single prolonged crisis but a whole series of psychic upheavals.[1] In between these he enjoyed, however, intervals of relative peace and well-being, when he devoted himself to painting or experiments in gold-making.

For a short time after his arrival in Paris Strindberg was a popular man in the literary circles of the city. But his rather hectic life led to ample consumption of absinthe, which did not greatly help his mental health. His scientific experiments gave him psoriasis, a painful eczema on his hands. He was haunted by financial difficulties and lived for certain periods of time on the charity of friends and acquaintances. On the verge of a crack-up he went to spend three weeks in the St. Louis Hospital in Paris. Although temporarily calmed by the maternal care of a nun in the hospital, he continued to have guilt feelings toward his former wives and children, whom he was not able to support. Prolonged periods of insomnia set in, and with his labile disposition Strindberg seemed caught in a vicious circle. He isolated himself more and more in a strange world of fears. Upset and exhausted, he began to feel "electric currents" through his body, and anxious to find their cause his paranoic mind, stimulated by his contact with French occultism, began to fabricate an explanation —he was being pursued by Scandinavian feminists and by a former friend, now his enemy, a Polish writer whom he had met in Berlin and who he now believed stood in telepathic rapport with "the powers," occult spirits who were out to torment him.

All the same, Strindberg did not plunge into a world of lunatic hallucinations. What restored him to mental health and new literary productivity was his gradual return to a personal faith in a divine order that he felt operated everywhere in life. Toward the end of his Inferno period he happened upon the writings of Emanuel Swedenborg [2] and he now came to see "the powers" as a form of Swedenborgian "corrective spirits" whose task it was to bring the proud writer and would-be scientist to a state of repentance through suffering and tribulation. From his journals one can surmise, however, that Strindberg had moved toward the position of a religious visionary even before he began to read the seventeenth-century Swedish mystic. What Strindberg borrowed from him was a certain terminology, but he reinterpreted Swedenborg's ideas to suit his own metaphysics. Thus Swedenborg's view of Hell became in Strindberg's new *Weltanschauung* the adequate description of life on earth, where human beings were chastened to be able to reach heaven. He found support for this view in his belief that certain topographical details in Swedenborg's description of Hell corresponded to the actual scenery of the region of Klam in Austria.

From now on Strindberg saw in the most everyday happening a message from another world, a warning, or an exhortation. He invested reality with a mystical power. Already in his scientific experiments he had been fascinated by medieval alchemy and black magic, and he had labored with a method of association and a theory of correspondences in such a way that the mutual combination of material objects took on a magic importance.

Now his wiping out of the final borderline between a scientific and mystical view of life resulted in a monistic belief that all objects and phenomena, visible and invisible, actual and dreamlike, hung together and fused. Later, via Schopenhauer, this belief was juxtaposed to the Neoplatonic and Vedic idea that life was an impure world, an imperfect image of a higher, ideal world. However, this philosophical conception was counterbalanced by a dualistic experiencing of existence, with roots in the sexual and moral conflict that underlay Strindberg's Inferno crises.

Strindberg now compared himself to a guilt-ridden Orestes, haunted by the Erinyes.[3] But he regarded his tribulations as expiatory sacrifices through which he would make amends for earlier evil deeds. His agonies seemed, however, so enormous to him as to outweigh his guilt many times; therefore the thought occurred to him that he was a man chosen by Providence to suffer also for the misdeeds of others. Having seen himself at one time as a proud rebel against God, he now assumed the role of mankind's *satisfactio vicaria*, of a divinely inspired visionary and supreme sufferer. His new position was in fact a kind of Nietzscheanism in reverse; but it can also be led back to his childhood pietism with its strong emphasis upon the innate evil of human nature and the sinful Fall of Man.

On the surface Strindberg's development from atheism to a religious conviction ran parallel to European cultural trends at the time. On the continent the naturalistic interest in science and documentation had steered toward new ideas of hypnotism in the 1880s and dissolved in occultism in the following decade. Many leading writers went through religious crises in the midnineties; they aroused public interest and were much discussed at the time. But although Strindberg's religious conversion was no doubt in part conditioned by the *Zeitgeist*, it was far from a mere cultural pose but was caused by his own agonies and psychic experiences. The central motivations behind his search for a divine power seem to have been his longing for protection, his growing need to recognize his own guilt without being crushed by it, and his desire to find an explanation for his personal and professional failures.

Strindberg remained a believer in a divine order to the end of his life even though his religious attitude fluctuated; states of deep repentance, humility, and resignation alternated with moments of bitter accusation and defiance, which he justified by claiming that God was not perfect but like everything else was in a state of evolution. It was, however, this very ambivalence that enabled Strindberg to project his metaphysical vision with such dramatic power. Another reason for the strong impact of Strindberg's post-Inferno drama can be found in the fact that Strindberg's vision differed from that of most other religious mystics in its secure anchoring in everyday reality. The world of such dramas as *A Dreamplay* or *The Ghost Sonata* is no mysterious never-never land; it is a world based on actual details but abstracted to the same degree as are the images and landscapes that appear to us in our dreams. This means that in a sense Strindberg never quite abandoned his sharp, naturalistic approach to reality; he merely gave it a new dimension. It is true that he was never again to recreate a given milieu with such meticulousness and immediacy as he had done in *The Red Room* or *The Natives of Hemsö*, but the concreteness of his post-Inferno works was nevertheless to be overwhelming.

Strindberg's eclectic faith had crystallized by the time he sat down to edit and expand the notes he had kept between 1893 and 1897. They were published in three volumes entitled *Inferno, Legends,* and *Jacob Wrestling.* Although based on the same psychic and religious experience, the three works differ somewhat in tone and approach.

Inferno is unique as a confessional work in that it describes the movement of a religiously oriented mind

rather than the state of a firm believer recapitulating
his past sins. Fundamentally this movement expresses
man's traditional longing for the world of the spirit.
But *Inferno* contains no visions of an afterlife, no ec-
static accounts of the marriage of body and soul. The
work describes, however, a *preparation* for a spiritual
state without physical encumbrances.

At the very opening of *Inferno* Strindberg rejoices at
his departure from his second wife and at his sexual
abstinence which fills him with a "feeling of psychic
purity, of manly virginity." Throughout his account
Strindberg has only contact with maternal, saintlike
women, such as his pious mother-in-law. His Beatrice
is safely reduced to a two-and-a-half-year-old girl, his
ethereal daughter Kerstin.

Opposed to this pure world of the spirit which knows
no sex, Strindberg sets up life on earth as the epitome of
dirt—"born with a nostalgia for heaven I cried like a
child at the dirt of existence." The impurity of life is
related—in what later became a familiar Freudian pattern—to the physical functions of man, to the intake of
food, to excretion, and to lovemaking. The name
Strindberg finally chooses for life on earth is Swedenborg's "excremental hell." Man and woman are, to
borrow a later phrase from the play *Advent*, "two cats
on a privy roof."

Throughout *Inferno* Strindberg is eager to emphasize
that his account is not based on hallucinations or airy
fantasies but on "observed phenomena." His primary
concern is not to convert others but to be believed. He
is haunted by the fear of the potential lunatic of being
declared mad. The final words of his *Inferno* attest to
this: "The reader who believes that this book is a fantasy
is invited to look at my diary, which I kept day after day
since 1895 and of which this work is merely an expanded and ordered excerpt."

Inferno ends surprisingly enough on a note of sus-

pended doubt. In *Legends,* on the other hand, Strindberg declares that having "placed himself alone in the
midst of the glowing heaps of Inferno," he can now
accept a position as moralizer and teacher. The book,
however, is a failure—its unctuous tone is irritating and
so insistent that one suspects Strindberg to be trying to
convince himself as well as others. The Eternal One,
who is rather vague and distant in *Inferno,* now emerges
as an Old Testament Jehovah. While Strindberg, in
earlier polemics against atheists, had likened God to
a shoemaker or watchmaker, he now calls him "a slinger
of stones." God is no longer a peaceful artisan but a
severe avenger and a threat.

Toward the end of 1897 Strindberg began working
on the third part of his *Inferno* suite. But *Jacob Wrestling* became no more than a fragment and was added
to later editions of *Legends.* It differs, however, so much
from that work that it should be treated separately.

The core of the book is a vision that the writer has
in the Luxembourg Gardens where he meets a Stranger,
apparently a Christ-figure, to whom he speaks a long
monologue filled with accusations, confessions, and attempts at self-justification. While *Inferno* conveyed the
image of a haunted man, and *Legends* emerged as a
compilation of testimonials set down to prove the presence of a divine power, *Jacob Wrestling* is defiant,
self-confident, and inquisitive, yet has a more quiet
rhythm than the earlier journals and transmits relatively
little of their anguish. The biblical references are numerous—Strindberg likens himself to Moses as well as
to Jacob and Job—but the Stranger to whom he addresses
himself is no severe punishing God-figure; rather, he is
a half-mocking creature in a pilgrim's frock, a concrete
image of the self-irony that occasionally broke through
in *Inferno.* In the end the Stranger refuses to furnish
Strindberg with the final answers and leaves him to his
own thoughts.

Toward the end of *Jacob Wrestling* Strindberg sees himself as a kin of Saul who, on his way to Damascus, was struck by God and converted to the apostle Paul. Out of this analogy grew the Damascus trilogy, which marked Strindberg's return to the theater and inaugurated an extremely productive period in his life. For the next four years he wrote an average of five dramas a year, and between 1897 and 1909 he published nearly half of his literary oeuvre—not all of it first-rate literature, but enough of it so as to make him one of the great innovators of modern fiction and, especially, drama.

6

Metaphysical Drama
From *To Damascus* to *The Great Highway*

The first play in the *To Damascus* trilogy was written in Paris in 1898 and should be regarded as an autonomous work. Several years (1898–1901) elapsed between the completion of the three dramas entitled *To Damascus*, and we know from Strindberg's correspondence at the time that he did not originally plan the first of these plays as part of a trilogy.

In the center of *To Damascus I* stands the Stranger, a writer who is financially and emotionally bankrupt. After meeting the Lady, her husband, and her parents, the Stranger leaves on a journey, is found ill and delirious in the mountains, and is taken to a religious asylum. Haunted by a bad conscience he sees his "victims" pass by in a feverish vision: he meets Caesar, the Fool who has gone mad "reading a certain author"; the Doctor with whose wife the Stranger has eloped; his parents whom he has neglected; a poor sister he has left in the lurch; two wives he has abandoned; but also the Beggar, his own double.

The Stranger is later reunited with the Lady. At the end he discovers that a registered letter, which he has refused to fetch, contains the money he has needed all along. In complaining over his poverty-stricken fate he has done the Invisible One a great injustice. The Lady now wants him to enter a church with her; the Stranger follows her but with hesitation, exclaiming half-defiantly: "Well, I can always go through; but I won't stay!"

To Damascus has usually been put in the same category as *A Dreamplay* and the later chamber plays. But the fact is that when Strindberg, in his 1904 preface to *A Dreamplay,* referred to *To Damascus* as "my earlier dream-play," the statement was an afterthought. At the time of its conception, *To Damascus* was for Strindberg *"a Lucky Per's Journey* set in our own time and based on reality." [1] Instead of emphasizing thematic unity as he was to do in *A Dreamplay,* Strindberg used the more conventional approach of unity through character.

Lucky Per's Journey had been one of Strindberg's most popular plays, and in 1896 it was revived at the Vasa Theatre in Stockholm as the first Swedish Strindberg production in many years. The success of this drama might have tempted the playwright to use a similar structure for *To Damascus;* after all, this play was to be Strindberg's attempt to reestablish himself in the realm of the theater. One might also recall that one of Strindberg's last dramas before the Inferno period was the kaleidoscopic *Keys of Heaven,* like *To Damascus* an educational pilgrimage drama.

Parallels certainly present themselves between *Lucky Per's Journey, Keys of Heaven,* and *To Damascus I*: all three plays employ a loose and flexible form; they deal with a man's struggle with his conscience and his gradual chastening; they suggest the Catholic church as a possibility for the seeker who, however, remains hesitant before this alternative. The basic philosophical mood is pessimistic in all three plays although the protagonist's final attitude is different in each drama, ranging from a belief in hard work (Lucky Per) to an acknowledgment of suffering as a prerequisite for salvation (the Stranger).

To Damascus I is designed as a station drama, that

is, the Stranger's stops along the way are places of expiation where he is tested and forced to contemplate his situation. The play opens and closes before the entrance of a church and the protagonist's journey describes a movement forward and back, with his stay at the asylum as a turning point. The scenes unroll themselves in calculated sequence and are reversed in the latter half of the play to show life's continuous repetition, a favorite idea of Strindberg's. In a letter that he sent to Geijerstam in March 1898 he wrote:

> The artful point lies in the composition, which symbolizes "the Repetition" that Kirekegaard talks about; the action unfolds itself toward the Asylum; there it knocks against the pricks and then kicks back, the pilgrimage, the turned lesson, the reiteration; and then it starts again at the same place where the playing ends and where it began. Perhaps you have not noticed how the settings unfold backwards from the Asylum, which is the back of the book that closes itself and encloses the action. Or like a snake biting its own tail.

To Damascus I is not a drama of conversion so much as a drama of struggling doubt. The Stranger's nightmarish vision in the asylum does not have the immediate impact of Saul's, his biblical prototype's, terrifying revelation on his way to Damascus. Yet, as stated in the letter above, Strindberg regarded the asylum scene as the high point of the drama, and he indicated this by casting it as a pure vision. It is a vision, however, that is realistically motivated, conditioned as it is by the protagonist's feverish state of mind. Through the Stranger's illness the spectator is forewarned of the complete shift from the real or half-real to the visionary, a crucial detail that separates *To Damascus I* from *A Dreamplay* and from later expressionist dramas.

The shift from reality to vision is also revealed in Strindberg's handling of the scenery, which is Naturalistic except in the asylum scene where a theatrical setting is used. The Fool, the Beggar, the Doctor, the Stranger's parents, two wives, and children sit around a table like a stylized group, all dressed in white. Strindberg adds in the stage direction: "over this, costumes of gauze in different colors. The faces waxen, white like corpses; and something ghostlike in their being and in their gestures."

The movement from an outer to an inner reality affects Strindberg's conception of the secondary characters in the drama. On one hand they are actual people whom the Stranger meets during his wanderings; on the other hand, they can be seen as projections of his wishes and fears. They offer alternatives to his present life, appear as warning examples, or loom as guilt-ridden monsters before him. Their role of imaginative dramatic images rather than independent characters stands in direct relation to the Stranger's own movement from the conscious to the subconscious level of his psyche. But whereas the Stranger, whose anonymity suggests a person who is a stand-in for all men, does not appear to be a flexible character, the other dramatis personae seem to "split and multiply," to borrow a statement from the preface to *A Dreamplay*. This has to do with their being, to some degree, either doubles or emanations of the Stranger's ego. Thus the female characters (the Lady and the Mother) often cease to be completely autonomous people; on such occasions they illustrate the two dichotomous functions of the Strindbergian woman: to save man from evil and to destroy pure, untainted love. The Lady accompanies the Stranger as a potential redeemer. The Mother ruins their relationship by tempting her daughter to read the Stranger's "evil" book.

In the early part of the play when the Lady is the

only woman present in the Stranger's sphere of reaction, he gives her the metonymic name of Eve, thus identifying her with Womankind. That the Lady at this point is more of a projection than an independent character emerges clearly in the following dialogue.

> THE STRANGER: . . . What are you crocheting?
>
> THE LADY: It's nothing, only a needlework.
>
> THE STRANGER: It looks like a net of nerves and ganglia in which your thoughts are caught. I imagine your brain to look something like that inside.
>
> THE LADY: I wish I had half the thoughts you want to ascribe to me, but I have none at all.
>
> THE STRANGER: Maybe that's why I like your company; why I find you so perfect that I can no longer imagine a life without you.

Since Freud, who began his career in a Vienna clinic at about the same time as Strindberg wrote *To Damascus I*, modern psychology has explained how we often choose to reenact our anxieties symbolically during our sleep and how we frequently do so with the help of imaginary or actually existing people with whom we identify. Quite independently Strindberg gave the Doppelgänger motif a similar modern framework. Although no doubt familiar with earlier occult conceptions of doubles (in *Inferno* he describes at some length his acquaintance with an American painter who is thought to be a reincarnation of the mesmerist Francis Schlatter), Strindberg does not approach the motif from any ghoulish angle; what makes his handling of the theme in *To Damascus I* so striking is that it becomes not an element of mysticism nor a mere symbolic effect, but an integral part of the Stranger's personal conflicts. Thus the Doctor, called the Werewolf by the Stranger although he hardly displays any beastlike qualities, is a character in whom the Stranger's fears of his own potential evil are consolidated. The Doctor "pursues" the Stranger, so that he sees his face along the rocky mountain path, in the very place where the Stranger meets his crisis and which he associates with Hell.

The Fool, called Caesar, and the Beggar are also reflections of fears within the protagonist. The former reminds him of painful incidents in his youth and of his potential megalomania ("caesarian madness"); the latter is the embodiment of his ambivalent attitude toward poverty—Strindberg feared decadence but also spoke of it occasionally as filling him with a sense of power. The feelings embodied in these two figures fuse in a later scene where the Stranger observes a madwoman in front of the poorhouse.

To Damascus I abounds in symbolic details often suggesting madness, decadence, and death, such as Caesar's preoccupation with the poinsetta, an "abnormal" flower that blooms in the cold of winter, and *timmermannen*, a bug mentioned at the funeral party in scene 1, whose ticking is associated with dying in Swedish folklore. In the crucial asylum scene the setting is reminiscent of a wake, and one wall is covered by a painting representing "the archangel Michael killing the Evil One." Together with Christian references (a rosary, a chapel) and metaphorical projections of life as a repetitious dream or nightmare (e.g., an evergrinding mill), the visual and auditory symbolism helps build up the composite mood of frustration and restlessness that permeates the Stranger's search and points forward to the ending of the play, which is an ironic rather than emotional catharsis. The Stranger reaches neither religious peace nor a convincing reconciliation with the Lady. It is hardly surprising that Strindberg later felt compelled to write a sequel to the play.

The dramatic action of *To Damascus II* opens with

a provocative argument by the Mother and the Lady whereby the Stranger's defiant attitude is rekindled. He now plunges into a disillusioning struggle of trying to win recognition and status among men; he attempts in vain to establish himself as a gold-maker. Gradually the Stranger learns that his suffering is God's just punishment of his *amour-propre*, and the Confessor leads him on a road of renunciation. Having given up all the temptations of the world, including his love for the Lady, the Stranger urges the Confessor to hurry toward a nonworldly refuge: "Come, priest, before I change my mind!"

The third play begins at the foot of a mountain where a white monastery is located, the goal of the Stranger's journey. His walk up the mountain is painful; he has to pass a phosphorous pond surrounded by syphilitic patients who are punished for having listened to the Stranger's views on morality. Among the victims is the Stranger's own son.

In a vision the Stranger sees the Lady transformed into his own mother but before he can reach her she disappears in a cloud. The Stranger realizes the impossibility of "redemption for mankind through woman." Even so, he returns once more to the foot of the mountain to marry again. But his experience is negative. Everything repeats itself. His children grow up to lose their innocence; his new wife changes from virgin bride to a sexual companion who fills him with disgust. As his marriage collapses, the Stranger discusses life between the sexes with the Tempter who leads the problem of strife and question of guilt all the way back to the Fall of Man. The only form of salvation open to the Stranger is to deny the world and enter a cloister. But it has to be a confessionless monastery; the Stranger retains his unwillingness to commit himself to a given religion; what he seeks is not a religious dogma but a haven of rest.

In *To Damascus I* the Stranger suffered guilt feelings for iniquities done to his family. In the second play he moves the moral reckoning to a social plane in that he upbraids himself for his vain scientific exploits. This culminates in the most remarkable scene of the play, the gold-maker banquet, a feast that changes from a pompous gesture of homage to a derisive spurning of the Stranger's gold-making efforts: one moment he is the guest of honor among formally dressed gentlemen; the next he finds himself ridiculed by drunken derelicts in a tavern.

But apart from the expressionistic gold-making celebration and its ignominious aftermath, which foreshadows the examination scene in A *Dreamplay*, *To Damascus II* is little more than a tedious rumination of old marriage motifs, filled with autobiographical references that do not blend well with the main action. The battle between the Stranger and his God subsides to allow Strindberg to air more tangible problems. Futile attempts are made to juxtapose these with the appearances of the Confessor, also called the Dominican and the Beggar. Having relegated the Lady to the realm of devils, Strindberg assigns the Confessor the role of corrective voice. He fails, however, to create any rapport between the Stranger and the Confessor; the latter simply comes forth as a mechanical lifelike instrument. In addition Strindberg gives him the disastrous ability to hypnotize the Stranger by means of distant gestures and looks. Such features threaten to pull *To Damascus II* down to the level of Grand Guignol.

To Damascus III indicates that the dramatic material had by now lost its visionary grip on Strindberg. The play is a desperate attempt to justify the Stranger's life, ending in a rationalized concoction of Swedenborgianism, Hegelianism, and the particular blend of misanthropy and resignation that characterizes most of

Strindberg's works from 1900 on. Isolated scenes like that of the phosphorous pond have a strong visual potential, but the play as a whole lacks theatrical verve and inner dynamics. Typical is the figure of the Tempter, who accompanies the Stranger throughout the play but remains little more than an allegorical fabrication, giving the play the same intellectualized quality as some of Eugene O'Neill's dramas about split personalities (e.g. *The Great God Brown, Days Without End*).

In *To Damascus III* the Stranger is no longer a haunted man trying to escape his guilty conscience. Strindberg has removed himself from his alter ego— a negative form of objectivity indicating that any absolute value judgments on an author's ability to transcend his personal feelings are of dubious importance. The Stranger now reviews his life, at first in a quarrelsome manner, later in a mood of quiet meditation, but never in the feverish anguish that marked his search in the two earlier Damascus plays.

Strindberg's experiences during the Inferno period continued to hold a grip on him. But the trend from inner agonizing struggle to a partly intellectualized and/or moralistic view of his situation, which was noticeable in both the Inferno journals and Damascus suite, can also be observed in the two plays, *Advent* and *There are Crimes and Crimes*, which he wrote during the winter 1898–99 and published under the common title *At a Higher Court*. In spite of their appearing in the same volume, the two dramas differ a great deal in milieu, tone, and dramatic composition.

Advent was originally planned as a children's play, partly inspired by the playwright's rereadings of Dickens and H. C. Andersen. Gradually, however, the mythic and supernatural elements of the fairy tale changed into a grotesque nightmare about an evil judge and his wife.

As the play opens, the judge and his wife sit in
their vineyard in front of a mausoleum built as a
dignified symbol of their lives. Their conversation is
pharisaical; they praise their own good fortune while
rejoicing at the misfortunes of others. But weird things
begin to happen: Death appears with his scythe; a
sailor with his head chopped off glides by in the dark;
the Devil, dressed as a poor schoolteacher, beats the
couple with a rod; a hailstorm destroys their harvest;
the judge's wife is taken to a ball among chalky-white
guests; the judge is brought before a court and condemned without a single person being present. In the
end the wife freezes to death in a marshland and the
judge is stoned to death by those he has condemned
unjustly.

The couple meet in Hell where they receive, as a
Christmas present, a children's peep-show theater in
which they can see their past and all their evil deeds.
Chastened at last, they discover the star of Advent and
see the manger with the Christ child.

Having completed *Advent*, Strindberg wrote in a letter to Geijerstam: "I have never been so uncertain as
to whether I have succeeded or failed." Theater producers have been equally hesitant, and the play was
not staged until 1915 in Munich, Germany. Four years
later the expressionist director Reinhardt set up the
play in Berlin. Oddly enough, scholars discussing the
prototypal importance of Strindberg for the expressionistic theater have paid very little attention to *Advent*.
And yet this play, to a much larger extent than *To
Damascus*, has the hysterical tone, macabre props, and
ghoulish atmosphere that characterize many expressionistic *Schreidramen*. Also, the handling of the dramatis
personae is basically expressionistic. The couple united
in their evil represents a central consciousness, and the
other characters emerge as a concretization of the

thoughts and fears of the couple, something that is
made clear by the wife when she asks in view of the
strange phenomena that take place: "Are these shadows
or ghosts or our own sick dreams?"

Strindberg once referred to *Advent* as "a Swedenborgian drama." The play has the stylized quality of
a work based on a theological doctrine rather than
character conflict. The judge and his wife demonstrate
the Swedenborgian thesis that the devil resides in lost
souls who pursue living people. But added to the Swedenborgian references is a new-testamental belief in
atonement through Christ, which connects *Advent* with
Strindberg's later, conventionally Christian dramas,
Easter and *The Bridal Crown*. Finally, Strindberg's
perennial philosophical companion Schopenhauer lends
his voice to the drama by proclaiming life as a vale
of suffering and expressing compassion for all human
beings—"Pity to you and pity to us all!"

In *There are Crimes and Crimes* Strindberg left out
the stark and excessive colors from *Advent* and produced a play that is taut in structure and relatively
disciplined in tone. The religious point of view is the
same in both dramas, but in *There are Crimes and
Crimes* Strindberg's moralistic zeal threatens to destroy
the dramatic tempo of the play and fill it with frequent
lectures and cants.

The basic weakness of the play can be led back to
Strindberg's conception of its main character, Maurice,
a playwright living in Paris. Maurice falls in love with
a sculptress, Henriette, and neglects his mistress, Jeanne,
with whom he has a small daughter. Wanting to be
free from responsibility so that he can devote himself
to Henriette, Maurice wishes his daughter dead. The
gods punish him at once. His child dies and he is
haunted by guilt but is also suspected of having murdered the girl. Henriette and his friends leave him, and

the performance of his play is postponed. But a new autopsy shows that Maurice's daughter died a natural death. An abbé who is the religious spokesman in the play frees Maurice morally: "When providence has given you absolution, I can add nothing." Maurice replies that he shall go to church "to settle this with myself —but tomorrow I shall go to the theater."

There are Crimes and Crimes is designed as a realistic drama, but its very realism proves detrimental to its success. Strindberg's rather primitive philosophical standpoint fits well into the macabre world of *Advent* but becomes almost ludicrous in a sophisticated Parisian milieu. Rather unpleasant to watch is the Swedenborgian machinery of retribution, which forms the religious core of the play and is manipulated by Strindberg in a self-defensive manner. The plot goes back to an incident during the Inferno crisis when Strindberg tried, by means of telepathy, to make his daughter Kerstin sick. Guilt feelings probably motivated him to write *There are Crimes and Crimes.* He designed it, however, as both a confession and an absolution but also justified the "happy end" to himself (and his editor) in claiming it to be a concession to the tastes of the Parisian public who demanded a light touch.

The triangle situation of *There are Crimes and Crimes* is certainly reminiscent of many boulevard comedies. But Maurice is handled with too much solemnity and subjective feeling for him to function as a comic character, although he shares with other characters in the genre a fatal blindness to his own self. But one suspects that this is quite unintentional on Strindberg's part; one gets the uncomfortable feeling that Strindberg failed to recognize Maurice's guilt feelings for what they are—a threat to his sensitive ego and a form of inverted self-pity.

Guilt as a dominant motivation often becomes a

central theme in Strindberg's post-Inferno production. Frequently he places the moral qualms of his characters within a Christian context. Two of his most successful dramas of this kind are *Easter* (1900) and *The Bridal Crown* (1901). In both of these the playwright juxtaposes individual wrongdoing and guilt with innocent or redemptive suffering.

In *Easter*, the main character is a Christlike person, Eleonora or "the Easter Girl," who returns from an asylum to her family in Lund. Her father (Heyst) is in prison for embezzlement of funds. The family, supported by Eleonora's proud brother Elis, a schoolteacher, is haunted by fear that the creditor Lindkvist shall appear upon the scene. The Easter Girl possesses the wisdom (rather than confusion) of the insane; her madness gives her a metaphysical dimension and sets her apart from most of the other dramatis personae, a fact of which she is naïvely aware, as when she confesses to Benjamin, the boy who lives with the Heyst family:

> For me there is neither time nor space. I am everywhere and of all times. I am in my father's prison and in my brother's schoolroom, I am in my mother's kitchen, and in my sister's shop, far away in America. . . . I was born old . . . I knew everything when I was born, and when I learnt anything, it was just like remembering. I knew all about people—their blindness and folly—when I was four years old.

Not long before he sat down to write *Easter*, Strindberg's favorite sister had been admitted to an asylum. Her fate seems to have been one of his deepest sources of inspiration, but in a letter he also mentions a literary prototype for Eleonora—the title figure in Balzac's novel *Seraphita*, an androgynous creature who is judged insane by ordinary people. Other literary soul mates of Eleonora's are the women figures in Maeterlinck's dramas (which had begun to interest Strindberg at this time), and Ibsen's young Hedvig in *The Wild Duck*. With the former the Easter Girl shares an ethereal hypersensitivity; with the latter an innocent precocity and an intuitive rapport with all of life.

The Christian connotations of Eleonora's destiny are, however, of Strindbergian origin. It is through Eleonora that *Easter* takes its place among Strindberg's "penitential dramas" with their characteristic movement from punishment-suffering to redemption. Eleonora expresses and embodies Strindberg's beliefs that an individual can atone, through voluntary sacrifice, for the crimes and sins of others, and that punishment is a grace of God.

Easter is a morality play in which the characters embody ethical positions which are intensified by a small-town atmosphere imbued with righteous thinking. Guilt is not only a private affair but is coupled with social shame and punishment. In a sense Eleonora's isolation is only a reflection of the fate of the rest of the Heyst household. The family is a group of social failures and outcasts: the mother huddles in the house cut off from any friends; Elis's sense of rejection leads him to believe he has lost his fiancée to another man; Benjamin, the boarder, fears ostracism after failing to pass the prestigious student examination.

The mood of social isolation and personal despair reaches its climax in act 2, on Good Friday. The dramatic action, which is rather slight, describes a movement comparable to the legendary Easter season. On Maundy Thursday there is a sense of impending disaster; on Good Friday a seeming deathblow is given to the family as Lindkvist, the creditor, appears in the neighborhood; on Easter Eve a mood of continued despair prevails as Elis is forced to review the case of his father. This is followed, however, by a happy ending in which Lindkvist, the creditor, plays a crucial role.

In creating concreteness around the anguished atmosphere of the Heyst home, Strindberg relies upon a technique reminiscent of the first part of *Gustav Vasa*. In Lindkvist he gives us a character who, like the Swedish king, hovers like an ominous but invisible ogre in the background and whose power and near presence is sensed by all. His footsteps are heard in the distance, his cane rasps, and his laughter echoes while his shadow and silhouette are projected against the drawn curtains of the Heyst house.

Lindkvist's role is to bring the family to moral insight. Upon his entrance at the end of the play he explains "the law of recurrence," the principle that all repeats itself, including one's good acts. Elis's father had once done Lindkvist a favor; therefore, he is in turn willing to overlook the family's debt to him.

Just as there was something diabolic about the offstage Lindkvist in the first half of the play, there is something divine about his final appearance. In an almost literal sense he functions as a *deus ex machina*. At first a Dickensian bogeyman, at last a celestial agent, Lindkvist belongs to the magical or supernatural sphere of the play. His clairvoyant and telepathic powers make him move closer to the world of Eleonora than to that of the other, more realistically conceived characters. *Easter*'s happy end may easily seem like a dramatic somersault, flaunting as it does any realistic conventions of credibility. What Strindberg is trying to do is to balance off middle-class verisimilitude, as represented by the Heyst household, with a belief in a divine order and a retributive scheme on earth, visualized in the corrective figure of Lindkvist. It is a dichotomy established earlier in the play between

Eleonora and her family. In a production of *Easter* the effect of the ending may well depend on the extent to which Lindkvist's role is integrated with that of the Easter Girl.

In the years around the turn of the century when an interest in folk traditions and folk psychology dominated much of Sweden's cultural life, the province of Dalarna, rich in history and native customs, became the inspirational locale and background for many painters and writers. It was in line with this trend that Strindberg wrote to painter Carl Larson in August 1900: "A big play about life in Dalarna has come over me, and I see it as something light and beautiful." Strindberg was referring to *The Bridal Crown*, but when the play was completed in January 1901 it had grown into a somber and tragic story set in the middle of the nineteenth century during the reign of King Charles XV.

It tells the story of young Kersti who has borne a son in secret but kills it to be able to marry Mats as a crown (virgin) bride. Plagued by a guilty conscience, Kersti confesses her crime on her wedding day and is thrown into prison. After meeting a Christlike child she attains peace of mind, but an old feeling of animosity between her family and that of Mats has flared up. Good feelings are not restored until after Kersti's death. She drowns early on an Easter Sunday as she is on her way from prison to church to expiate her sin.

Together with his next play *Swanwhite, The Bridal Crown* is Strindberg's most stylized and lyrical drama. Its source of inspiration is to be found in Swedish folk ballads, more specifically in the antiphonal songs between a shepherd boy and a shepherd girl which Strindberg knew from Richard Dübeck's *Svenska vallvisor och hornlåtar*. Strindberg himself contributed one composition to the play, the melancholy and monotonous song of the Neck (water-sprite).

The Bridal Crown penetrates beyond the folk allusions of its Dalecarlian painted backdrop and conveys something of the dark lyricism and mythic anchoring of Swedish country traditions. Its rhythmic dialogue makes no attempt to reproduce a provincial idiom, but its slightly archaic tone is in keeping with the legendary material that Strindberg uses and reinforces the magical atmosphere of the play. Thematically *The Bridal Crown* dramatizes a relatively common thought in Strindberg's post-Inferno outlook: the redemptive power of certain individuals. But unlike, for instance, King Magnus in *The Saga of the Folkungs* and Eleonora in *Easter*, Kersti is a moral agent in her own right; and *The Bridal Crown* tells first and foremost of her personal destiny, of her hardened ambitions leading to the murder of the child, of her agonized conscience, materialized in her visions of specters and mythical figures, and of her final atonement for the crime.

In order for her destiny to purge society—here represented by the two rival families—Kersti's character must have stature and symbolic potential. Strindberg achieves this by casting her as a person of passion, strength, and willpower, somewhat reminiscent of the women in the old Norse sagas. But Kersti lives not only in the stark and romantic world of folk legend; the moral values of the play are Christian, with a particular reference to the Book of Job. It is Strindberg's successful fusion of legendary and Christian sources that makes *The Bridal Crown* quite unique in his dramatic production.

Swanwhite, written a few months after *The Bridal Crown*, retains much of the fatalistic quality of Kersti's drama but loses its earthy attributes. Instead the mood is ethereal, designed to sustain its main theme, the purity of self-sacrificing love, or what Strindberg summarized in a letter to actress Anna Flygare as "Caritas, the great Love that suffers all and survives all; that forgives, hopes, believes—even after all has failed!"

The literary model for *Swanwhite* can be found in medieval courtly ballads and in Maeterlinck's *Madeleine* and *Le trésor des humbles*. Strindberg's fresh and untainted love for the young actress Harriet Bosse, who was to become his third wife and to whom he presented *Swanwhite* as an engagement gift, made him susceptible both to Maeterlinck's worship of spiritual beauty and to his lyrical twilight moods. He was also drawn to the idealization of nonsexual love found in the songs of the troubadours. But the dramatic result —a hybrid between fairy play and idealized domestic drama—did not prove to be Strindberg's forte. In spite of its poetic qualities, *Swanwhite*'s tone of timid naïveté is not in keeping with Strindberg's dramatic talent. Its lyrical passages point forward, however, to A *Dreamplay*, which he published in 1901.

Two days before he finished his *Dreamplay* Strindberg wrote in his diary:

> Am reading about the teachings of Indian religion. The whole world just a mirage.—The divine primal power let himself be seduced by Maya or the urge to propagate. Hereby the divine element sinned against itself (love is sin; hence, the agonies of love constitute the greatest hell there is). Thus the world exists only through a sin, if it exists at all—for it is only a dream vision (hence my Dreamplay a vision of life), a phantom the destruction of which is the task of asceticism. But this task enters into conflict with the urge to make love, and the sum total is an endless wavering between the pleasure of love and the agony of penance!

The excerpt above is in part incorporated into the ending of A *Dreamplay* and into the prologue, added five years later. But the play as a whole, with its tension between dream (life) and reality (death-awakening), body and spirit, sexuality and asceticism, makes it clear that Strindberg's chance reading in Indian philosophy brought about a confirmation of ideas he had already dramatized in the play rather than a new revelation.

The loosely-constructed plot of A *Dreamplay* tells of how the daughter of the Indian God Indra descends to earth to learn of the plights of man. As in a dream Indra's daughter is brought to the imprisoned Officer in a strangely growing castle. Later she assumes the role of concierge at the Opera and watches the Officer wait for his beloved Victoria until he grows old and his bouquet of flowers has withered to a bunch of dry sticks. She marries a Lawyer who takes upon himself the sufferings of his clients but cannot live in harmony with a woman. She visits Fairhaven whose owner is blind and Foulstrand where young lovers suffer and ugly Edith is spurned although she can play Bach so beautifully that all have to stop and listen.

Indra's daughter also witnesses an absurd doctoral ceremony and the Officer's humiliating examination when he fails the simplest questions in arithmetic. She watches the social injustice among coal heavers on the luxurious Riviera, and she listens together with the Poet to the elegiac singing of the winds and the waves in Fingal's Cave. Carrying with her the lament of the Poet, she finally ascends to heaven.

A *Dreamplay* follows the pattern of Strindberg's earlier "wayfaring" or pilgrimage dramas, with kaleidoscopic groups of people and constantly shifting scenes. But it employs the polyphonic form in a new and, for modern drama, revolutionary way. Its nondimensional structure, says Strindberg in the famous preface to the play, follows the outline of a dream in which "time and space do not exist." Above all the characters, male as well as female, stands "one consciousness, that of the dreamer," whom many critics have identified with the transmutative Indra's daughter. Through her "the winding tale" which is the dream moves gradually from a psychological to a metaphysical level and expands from an individual nightmare to a transcendental vision of life.

But it is also possible to see the dreamer as an invisible bisexual psyche projecting its extended experience of life through a number of dramatis personae, who together form a composite picture of Man and Woman. Or one might simply link the dreamer with Strindberg as the creator of the drama, an approach that would find support in the playwright's frequent references to himself as a godlike observer and all-encompassing seer. But it is an interpretation that has laid the play open to criticism. Strindberg as the dreamer, says Raymond Williams, "is machinery rather than substance." [2] A reading that precludes a participating fictional dreamer seems also to raise the question of the drama's coherence. Is there a unifying element that is capable of containing in itself all the aspects of the invisible dreamer's vision? John Gassner and John R. Milton [3] feel that this is not the case and that the drama remains a subjectively confusing, intellectual demonstration. Evert Sprinchorn, on the other hand, has pointed to the erotic imagery of the play as a cohesive factor. [4]

Strindberg himself may have had certain qualms about the efficacy of his dream-play form. Perhaps it dictated his addition of the prologue in which Indra's daughter speaks to her father before descending on earth. Since *A Dreamplay* ends with the departure of

Indra's daughter from earth, Strindberg possibly intended the prologue to give unity to his drama through
one of his favorite dramatic designs, the circular structure.

But perhaps most of our difficulty in approaching
A *Dreamplay* stems from our lack of dramatic precedent,
for here is a play that breaks the agelong tradition of
conceptual drama. In order to facilitate the transcen-
dency of the self in the theater, Strindberg created a
new drama which is theme-centered, abstract, visual,
and distorted. As in our dreams, the emphasis lies on
association of ideas rather than construction of a plot
based on logical connection of cause and effect. The
method, however, does not necessarily leave out an
intellectual arrangement of the dramatic material. A
Dreamplay is certainly not the result of "spontaneous
writing" but, on the contrary, was unusually slow in
completion. Thus the various drafts reveal that the
fusion of Schopenhauer, Swedenborg, Indian mysticism,
and reminiscences of the Inferno experience, which
forms the philosophical and poetic core of the drama,
occurred only gradually.

By casting the whole of life as an agonizing dream,
did Strindberg succeed in transforming his personal
suffering into a universal vision? His splitting of the
male and female into many characters certainly enabled him to put forward a much more unbiased and
complex view of the two sexes than in his earlier works.
Indra's daughter portrays woman as a maternal con-
soler when she dons the shawl of the concierge and
receives the testimonies of all those who suffer. But
as a wife she embodies sexuality, that is, tainted love.
Married to the Lawyer she has to reenact a typical
Strindbergian marriage, in which petty irritations assume catastrophic proportions. Finally Indra's daughter
plays the role of mediary between man and God, a

role which is ancient in history, woman being by tradition associated with the church.

Strindberg's portrait of man shows him to be the eternal child. The Officer is confronted with his mother and chastised by her; he relives the injustices of his childhood, and even after he has received a doctor's degree he sees himself as a child facing an absurd examination. Man also assumes his traditional intellectual role in society—all four members of the faculties are men. But man engaged in intellectual pursuit is now being satirized, in contrast to the respect with which the type was being treated in Strindberg's dramas of the 1880s. The playwright's admiration and sympathy lie with man in his role as *satisfactio vicaria* (the Lawyer) and as an artist—the Poet gets more of Strindberg's attention the closer the play is brought to a resolution of its many disparate elements.

The Lawyer and the Poet—as well as the Officer with his Platonic love for Victoria—are presented to us as men who aspire to a spiritual life but are placed in a world full of the challenge and agony of sexuality. Nowhere in the play does this receive a more poignant expression than in the image of the growing Castle rooted in the soil. The Officer, haunted by his Shelleyan "desire of the moth for the star," is imprisoned in the Castle where he complains about having to "groom horses, clean stables and have the muck removed." But when Indra's daughter finds the Officer, he only hesitantly permits her to lead him out of the Castle. His fears are not unfounded: just outside the gate of the Castle he sees a giant monkshood—with its poisonous root a traditional symbol of worldly desire. By now Indra's daughter has assumed the traits of an earthly woman. Going with her the Officer, as later the Lawyer, experiences the essential dichotomy in life between the body and the soul: man's hope to be redeemed by woman turns into a realization that woman as an earthbound creature can only thwart his spirit since he is drawn to her by physical attraction, culminating in sexual contact.

For all its metaphysical implications, Strindberg's vision of life was dictated by his repulsion at physical intimacy, which reveals itself in his many references to the procreative process as a filthy act. In A *Dreamplay* the phallus-shaped Castle harboring the spiritual but growing out of manure—a microcosm of the physical nurtured by excremental dirt—becomes an overpowering stage image of Strindberg's negative view of sex.

Yet Strindberg's physical nausea is expressed not only in sexual metaphors but in his grotesque or contemptuous approach to those who ignore the spiritual aspirations of men. In one of the most astonishingly absurdist scenes in the play, Agnes and the Lawyer, who both seek the absolute (the Lawyer in his Christlike role and Agnes as Indra's daughter) are shut within the four walls of their home by the pedestrian servant Kristin, who spends all her time at the menial task of pasting doors and windows.

Finally the Poet offers us a sarcastic version of the frustrating dualism of human life. The spirit can survive (but not be freed) if one hardens one's skin by "wallowing in the mire." An attitude of mocking irony may be the answer to "the stinging gadflies" of earthbound men. Yet of the men in A *Dreamplay* the Poet comes closest to resolving the conflict between body and soul. When he enters the Cave with Indra's daughter, Strindberg suggests once more the encounter of body and spirit on earth. But the Poet resists the destruction of the body; when asked if he does not want to be "released" he abstains. Once more he "gets homesick for the mud." The Poet, the visionary who can communicate the transcendental, is nevertheless compelled to stay on earth. And mankind as a whole —here represented by the crew of a sinking ship seen by the Poet and Indra's daughter—screams in fear of their deathly "Redeemer." It becomes the fate of Indra's daughter to face voluntarily the actual annihilation of the body, the only thing that can bring permanent peace, for sexual abstinence is not enough to obliterate evil. Strindberg's transposition of the problem of evil from a moral-puritanical to a metaphysical plane culminates as Indra's daughter enters once more the growing Castle which now bursts into flames, a purifying fire out of which blooms the giant chrysanthemum, traditional flower of peace and spirit in Oriental mythology.

But before she can leave life on earth behind, Indra's daughter must free herself from that which binds her to life among human beings, even to the point of abandoning her own child; and she must perform the final task of opening a mysterious door, which is thought to harbor the secret of existence. The door, however, reveals nothing; mortal man can surmise but not attain full cognizance of the transcendental. Yet he will continue to present suppositions of the meaning of the mystery; Indra's daughter leaves the members of the four faculties behind, each one of them arguing his interpretation of the empty space behind the opened door.

The major thrust of *A Dreamplay* follows the journey of Indra's daughter. Yet basically the dramatic design is not conceived as a forward movement in space but as a series of concentric circles describing the ever-widening scope of the theme of discord and disharmony. This is first seen in the interaction of individuals, where one person's good deed or happiness is often the source of another's misery and discontent (exemplified for instance in the Mother giving her shawl to a servant but in doing so, arousing the displeasure of her husband).

Conflict and imbalance reach societal proportions in scenes depicting professional bickering (e.g., Lawyer's fate and meeting of four faculties) and social injustice (e.g., coal heavers on the Riviera). And finally Indra's daughter—her intonation of "Man is to be pitied" [Det är synd om människorna] reaching its painful crescendo—suggests the universal presence of irreconcilable forces which underlie all human relationships and seem woven into the very fabric of life.

Thus conflict, the very basis of all dramatic writing, is also by now the essence of Strindberg's dichotomous *Weltanschauung*, summed up by Indra's daughter at the end of the play in words whose undulating rhythm is juxtaposed to the jarring and piercing sound of the last line ("motsats, obeslutsamhet, disharmoni"):

> *Oh, now I know the pain of all existence.*
> *This, then it is to be a human being . . .*
> *To miss the things one never prized*
> *and feel remorse for what one never did . . .*
> *To wish to go, yet long to stay . . .*
> *And so the human heart is ripped in two,*
> *emotions seem by horses torn,*
> *in conflict, irresolution and disharmony.*

At the end of his preface to A *Dreamplay* Strindberg writes: "As for the loose, disconnected form in the drama, it is only seemingly so. For at a closer examination, the composition is found to be quite firm—a symphony, polyphonic, fugued here and there with the main motif still returning, repeated and varied by the some and thirty voices in all tonal keys." The interest he expresses here in an analogy between drama and music culminated for Strindberg in his so-called chamber plays, which he wrote for his own Intimate Theatre in 1907–8.

Two years prior to Strindberg's realization of his life-

long ambition to have a stage of his own the tide had
begun to turn for him. *The Dance of Death* had been
well received in Germany in the fall of 1905. In the
next season *Creditors* and *There are Crimes and Crimes*
were produced with relative success in Stockholm, while
Miss Julie went on the road, under the leadership of the
director August Falck. Plans were under way to present
Gustav Vasa, A Dreamplay, and *Lucky Per's Journey* in
the Swedish capital. By the early part of 1907 August
Strindberg was again a respected name in Swedish
theater circles.

Falck's version of *Miss Julie* had aroused a particular
interest among the public. This fact plus the young
director's magic combination of Christian and family
name (Falk being the name of Strindberg's alter ego in
The Red Room) made the somewhat superstitious
Strindberg especially amenable to a suggestion by
August Falck that the two of them start a theater of
their own. In a matter of months they had assembled
an enthusiastic ensemble, created a new stage in a re-
modeled store seating 161 persons, and produced the
first of five chamber plays which Strindberg wrote especially for the company.

A year earlier the famous German director Reinhardt
had started his Kammerspielhaus in Berlin. This probably served as an outer impulse for Strindberg to form
his own small and intimate stage. But the basic idea
was really a revival of Antoine's Théâtre Libre program
from the 1880s. In all likelihood the great success of
Miss Julie in 1906 led Strindberg's thoughts back to the
time when the *quart d'heure,* the concentrated, uninter-
rupted piece of drama, was fashionable. A letter from
the early part of 1907 indicates that in his new plays he
intended to revive the dramatic pattern of *Miss Julie*
and *Creditors*; he called again for a drama with "a
small theme dealt with in detail, few people, . . . no

big apparatus, no superfluous secondary characters, . . .
no drawn-out full evenings." A year later Strindberg
stated to August Falck that "two chairs and a table—
that's the ideal," an asceticism in decor that definitely
echoes *Creditors*.

But as time went on, Strindberg's new program became much less definite and precise. In 1908, having
completed his chamber plays, he was anxious to emphasize that "no particular form shall bind the author, for
the theme dictates the form." On the same occasion he
began to refer to his plays as sonatas and revealed his intention to transpose "the idea of chamber music to
drama." He did not, however, proceed to explain in
exact terms the relationship between his dramatic approach and the chamber music form. He seems to have
had in mind the sonatas of Beethoven, his favorite
composer, but we have no real indication that he followed their structure in more than a general way; his
chamber plays possess somewhat of the antiphonal
quality and thematic parallelism of Beethoven's music,
and they reveal an ambition to evoke a mood rather
than develop a dramatic plot. Yet, Strindberg's Opus 1
to 5—*Stormy Weather, The Burned House, The Ghost
Sonata, The Pelican,* and *The Black Glove*—show that
the playwright departed from his attempts to make
literature approximate music in that he relied upon a
subject matter which, although conceived visually, suggested an intellectual process and aimed at re-creating
a metaphysical rather than purely emotional image of
life.

In Strindberg's chamber plays, which proved to be
very much the drama of the future, the spectator finds
little of conventional character development. The
emphasis is on the setting and its impact upon the
dramatis personae; as Rinman so succinctly has said:
"houses, not people . . . are the central characters." [5]

These houses when viewed from the outside seem respectable enough but upon closer scrutiny they turn out to harbor hidden evils. Except in *The Pelican*, evil is not limited to a specific individual but is a state of mind permeating an entire milieu and affecting those who live in it. The drama unfolds when an outsider enters into such an environment. Then we look behind the scenes: doors open into strange rooms; self-made roles disintegrate; and voices speak up bringing back suppressed memories, revealing the guilty past, or foreshadowing an agonizing future.

The houses and buildings in the chamber plays have then the same metaphorical function as the growing castle in *A Dreamplay*: they represent life on earth in its never-ending tension between body and spirit, appearance and reality. We see its outer façade of deceit and pretension as well as its core, the human conscience experiencing shame and guilt before the inner ugliness of mankind. The dramatic action takes the form of a day of unmasking when individuals are brought to recognize their misery in being born or have to reap the result of their misdeeds. When the illusions fall, the people wake up as from an evil dream. But the telling of the truth paves the way to death; for some the end is a suicidal punishment, for others it is a liberation from agony.

The setting of the first of the chamber plays, *Stormy Weather*, is an ordinary house in the fashionable section of Stockholm. In one of the apartments an old gentleman lives alone, attended by a young servant. His brother, a Consul, comes to visit and reveals the identity of the new tenants in an apartment upstairs. They are Gerda, the old gentleman's former wife, and her new husband who has formed a club and is responsible for the nightly orgies that rock the house; staying with them is Gerda's child from her previous marriage. When her present husband beats her and threatens to exploit a confectioner's teenage daughter, Gerda asks the old gentleman to rescue her. He rejects her but with the help of the Consul he manages to undo her husband's scheme. Gerda and the child depart.

Stormy Weather was written shortly after Harriet Bosse had left Strindberg and was planning to remarry. A letter Strindberg sent to Miss Bosse after the opening of the play reveals its biographical anchoring: "You are angry with me because of a play you saw at the Intimate Theatre. I had warned you about it! For it was a painful fable, with which I wanted to write you and our little one out of my heart! I wanted to take out in advance the agonies that awaited me." Actually Strindberg seems to have been more anxious to indulge in a kind of revenge fantasy, as he belittles his passion and reduces its object to an unattractive, clinging trollop. The crucial confrontation scene also enables him to depict himself as superior in every way to his successor.

Yet, Strindberg's ultimate concern is not the old gentleman's requital but his final settlement with life itself. He is not presented to us as a pathetic cuckold but as an old man whose peaceful resignation is threatened by memories of the past. He spends his days with pleasant trifles—a game of chess, small talk with the confectioner downstairs, routine walks through the neighborhood. His belief is that the best life is one with "no love, no friends, just a bit of company in our loneliness; then people can just be people, without any claim on our feelings or sympathies; then one feels oneself growing loose like an old tooth, and one drops out with neither pain nor a sense of loss."

The old man's rejection of physical contact is a preparation for death—he announces at the end his decision to leave the house, where he has lived to see both weddings and funerals. There are numerous allusions in the play to the house as a place for old people who have withdrawn from life. It is called The Silent House; at one time it was in part a nursing home, outside which wagons would stop at night to fetch the corpses of those who had died; the confectioner's business is poor and he is advised to move but is too tired to change his quarters; earlier in the summer a tenant upstairs has died in a fever. The young people move away; the rest of the tenants are never seen, but in one window a palm tree throws a shadow on the curtains "like an iron funeral spray."

Although resigned, deep down the old man harbors a buried restlessness; he is waiting for something to happen, for a storm to break out. The silent but sultry air outside is a metaphor for his anxious state of mind. But the oppressive calm and rumbling thunder in the first half of *Stormy Weather* accentuate a tension of which *all* the characters partake. They are quiet as shadows, listening more than speaking, and they wait rather than act until the thunderstorm has cleared the air. Shortly afterward when the first street lamp is lit as a sign of the end of a summer that has been unusual in its suffocating heat, the old man, too, is finally purged of passion and ready to depart.

"One is supposed to touch nicely on their filth," says the old man in *Stormy Weather* after his meeting with the people upstairs. In his next play, *The Burned House*, Strindberg shows no such scruples in revealing the corrupt nature of mankind. In depicting his acrimonious view of life he uses as his spokesman the Stranger, who returns after thirty years in America to the house of his childhood only to find that it has just burned down. Among those who have occupied it is the materialistic Dyer, the Stranger's brother, whose wife has had an amorous affair with a student lodger. The Dyer makes the Student appear to have started the fire

(which apparently was accidental) and he is arrested
for arson.

The Stranger has the unmasking powers which Strindberg himself claimed to possess. He soon reveals that
the burned house has always been a microcosm of lies
and deceits. It is located in a neighbourhood called "The
Swamp" where everybody "fights all the time and back-
bites." The Stranger once left home because he was
falsely accused of being a seducer. For some time he
retained high thoughts of his family, but once on a train
in South Carolina he met a friend from home who
disclosed the truth about his parents: they were smug-
glers using their house to hide the contraband in.

The disillusionment experienced by the Stranger on
this occasion seems to contradict his alleged indifference
to his family, stemming from a suicidal attempt at the
age of twelve: "I took life with cynical calmness. . . .
My family? I've never felt myself to be a relation of you
people." Certain things indicate, in fact, that the
Stranger's stated aloofness to the world around him is
in part a rationalized attitude. Hearing him—and the
play is largely a series of monologues—one keeps thinking of Strindberg the detached artist and perennially
injured man who never forgot a wrong done to him.
The Stranger's ambiguity takes the form of hateful
(rather than calm) denunciations of his family and of
all mankind: "If we wanted to be just, we could put a
rope around the neck of the whole family of man. . . .
It's a terrible family: ugly, sweaty, stinking, dirty linen,
filthy socks with holes, sores, bunions, ugh! . . . One
must be a pig to feel at home in this mush."

In the course of the play it transpires that most of
the people in the neighborhood are related; the community, with the burned house as its center, is an image
of guilt-ridden mankind. As in *Stormy Weather* the
panorama of life is being suggested; a wedding is planned
at the same time as the prospective father-in-law

(Gustavsson) is making a wreath because "something is going on up at the cemetery." The cycle of life is embodied in Mrs. Vesterlund, the Dyer's old nursemaid and now the owner of a tavern called The Coffin Nail, "where the hearses pull up, and the condemned men used to get their last glass on the way to the gallows."

The Burned House is above all the Stranger's synopsis of life. Most of the decisive events have taken place when the drama begins. But woven into the Stranger's philosophical meanderings we find a subplot, the search for the cause of the fire. In the end the case is dismissed for lack of evidence. The detective plot has a certain relevance to the Stranger (although it seems to be independent of his moves), for it supports his view of a secret unknown plan of which an ordinary human is unaware but which he as a visionary can surmise; from his array of experiences he has arrived at a fatalistic position and a belief in "the World Weaver" (which was also the original title of the play); he sees "a coherence, a repetition" in everything.

In telling his brother, the Dyer, of his reactions at the discovery of his family's criminal nature, the Stranger says:

> Now I had to redesign their faces, strip them naked, pull them down, put them out of my mind. It was terrible! Then, later, *they began to haunt me. The pieces of the shattered figures reassembled themselves, but they didn't fit together properly any more. They became a chamber of horrors.* . . . All those nice gray-haired old men who came to our house and whom we called uncles, who played cards and took late suppers with us—they were all smugglers and some had worn handcuffs. (Italics mine.)

The Stranger's statement might be said to contain the nucleus of *The Ghost Sonata*, a play written almost simultaneously with *The Burned House*. It is a drama which is also concerned with the unmasking of a sham world, but its vision is more grotesque, exposing a house which upon closer look becomes a hallucinating chamber of horrors. The way in which Strindberg achieves this effect is through a style that employs dramatic metaphors in a surrealistic way, carrying the technique from *A Dreamplay* one step further; not satisfied with projecting *les misères de la vie* by using the *structure* of a dream, Strindberg recreates in *The Ghost Sonata* the entire, absurd *world* of a dream, in which people act out their destructiveness and evil without the bridling influence of their superegos.

Strindberg referred to *The Ghost Sonata* as "a world of intimations." In it move a Student of philology, who has just carried out a heroic rescue, and an old crippled man, Hummel; the two meet outside a fashionable house. Hummel enables the Student, a so-called Sunday child with second sight, to enter the house and make the acquaintance of a young woman, Adèle or the Hyacinth Girl, who is really Hummel's illegitimate daughter. The house turns out to be full of strange characters; among them is a Mummy who lives in a closet and a Cook who serves only overcooked, tasteless food. The climax of the play is a ghost supper at which the specter-like guests, including Hummel, are unmasked. After his crimes are revealed Hummel goes into the Mummy's closet to hang himself. The Student now discovers that Adèle is deathly ill and that he himself is being poisoned by the atmosphere in the house.

Although Strindberg employs a retrospective technique on the surface reminiscent of Ibsen's in its gradual unfolding of the past, he is not concerned with his characters' search for moral integrity but with a presentation of life as a web of irrevocable and partly suppressed guilt. The evil he projects and suggests on the stage may be calculating and personal as in

Hummel's case but it is also existential, the original
sin of which all human beings partake. In revealing
how also the pure at heart like the Hyacinth Girl and
the Student must needs be tainted by "the dirt of life,"
Strindberg lets *The Ghost Sonata* develop not in the
logical progression of an Ibsen play but by the same
associative and strongly visual pattern he employed in
A Dreamplay. This technique, depending for its plausibility on subconscious levels of reality, achieves coherence by its reliance upon thematic rather than psychological progression. Here the play's relation to musical
structure is important. *The Ghost Sonata* was written
with Strindberg's favorite Beethoven sonata in mind
(opus 31, no. 2 in D major) and divided into three
movements (scenes) according to the musical form
ABA. Scenes 1 and 3 concern the Student's confrontation with the world of the play; scene 2 in which the
Student takes no active part deals with the guests at the
ghost supper and their unmasking. Finally, the Student
brings the play to a close by a restatement and summing-
up ("the coda") of its major themes: he tells the story
of his father's "ghost supper" when he (the father) revealed the truth and was destroyed by it; and he con-
cludes that death is the only relief from the pain of
living.

The musical structure with its variation and reitera-
tion of themes was much more than a technical device
to Strindberg; it was a form that lent itself to his basic
belief that human life followed a pattern of repetition,
which he had already tried to dramatize in, for instance,
The Dance of Death, and had suggested again toward
the end of *The Burned House* as he brought two young
lovers onto the stage only to have them begin to relive
the fate of the main participants in the drama.

In dramatizing the main theme of *The Ghost Sonata*
—the pervasive power of evil which destroys innocent

and guilty alike—Strindberg reduces life in society to its most elemental and demanding level, the family. All the people in the house are related mysteriously as well as biologically, including the Cook who belongs "to the Hummel family of vampires" and the Student who enters the house as Hummel's prospective son-in-law. The evil of this family collective expresses itself in its number of adulterous and illegitimate relations but reaches its most powerful manifestation in the vampire motif, which is skillfully woven into the dramatic texture of the play. Hummel himself, as leader of the clan, is a master exploiter whose power extends beyond the walls of the house; he has bribed the police to give him criminal news which he might be able to use for his own purposes. Although he is a paralytic wreck of a man, he creates the impression of a dictator; when he sits in his wheelchair he is likened to the heathen god Thor riding his chariot across the skies. Accompanied by beggars and ruffians, poor gossipers and informers of the city, Hummel emerges as an image of the miser, the busybody, and the usurper. It is only fitting that his former occupation was that of a loan shark, a profession whereby one lives off the interest of others. Something of Hummel's sponging nature may also be implied in his very name, which suggests the Swedish word *humla*, bumblebee.[6] Hummel certainly gives the impression of a sucking and constantly buzzing insect.

The vampire theme is extended to the scene of the ghost supper, a meager meal disguised as an ostentatious ceremony, where the attending guests have apparently sucked strength from each other for years until they are now mere living shadows, as weakened as the tea they sip. The motif culminates in the last scene with the appearance of the Cook, who is likened by the Student to "one of those lamias that suck the blood of suckling babes" and who has swelled into an enormous ogre stuffing herself on the food meant for the family.

Within the world of the ghostlike house the Student's role is ambivalent; he is both participant and observer, explorer and recorder. Like Indra's daughter in A *Dreamplay* and the Stranger in *The Burned House*, he is drawn into the action, yet retains certain traits which at the beginning of the play make us associate him with an idealistic and transcendental realm: his early encounter with the Milkmaid at the fountain has Christian overtones (cf. Gospel of St. John, chapter 4, in which Jesus asks a Samaritan woman for water); his clairvoyance enables him to see the Milkmaid, visible only to the innocent or rueful; and during his first appearance on the stage, church bells begin to chime.

The descent of Indra's daughter took her on a journey through life; the Student, in entering the Hummel house, sets out on a similar journey, through a house designed as a metaphor for life. At the end, the Student, having been initiated into both the horrors and nasty triviality of living, finds that he can only preserve his purity by leaving the ghost house behind and addressing himself to the divine power whose presence was vaguely suggested in the first scene and who now is identified with the spirit of Buddha.

The people in *The Ghost Sonata* all move into the realm of death, suggested by the Student's last speech and by the final projection of Böcklin's picture *Isle of the Dead*. Strindberg tried to write a sequel, called "Toten-Insel," but failed to complete it; once the problem of evil and suffering had moved out of the world of the living, it seemed to lose dramatic potential.

Strindberg could not, however, let go of the problem. In *The Pelican*, the fourth of his chamber plays, he took it up anew but let the action revolve around the survivors of the dead man who had been the central character in the Toten-Insel fragment. In the center of the action stands a widow who pretends to be a loving mother but is revealed to be a vampire, feeding on her two children. She has also forced a bankrupt lieutenant to marry her daughter. The son, a drunkard, sets fire to their house. The mother jumps out of a window and is killed, while son and daughter die in each other's arms, consumed by the flames.

The Pelican may be regarded as a variation of Strindberg's short play *Mother Love* from the 1880s. Its title is equally ironic: the pelican bird is said to give of its own blood to sustain its young ones. In Strindberg's play the mother does the very opposite. She is a reincarnation of the Cook in *The Ghost Sonata*; her children are undernourished because, for years, their mother has fed them diluted and artificially seasoned food. Now the children are caught in a vicious circle: they are weak because they have been starved, and because they are weak, they cannot free themselves from their torturer. The mother, in turn, has become as puffed up as a frog, fat and ugly from all the food she has stuffed herself on; she nevertheless believes herself to be young and attractive. But her guilty conscience plagues her in the form of nightmarish fears. Seeing the red sofa where her husband used to sit, the pelican mother thinks of it as a slaughter bench. The legs of the rocking chair create in her mind an image of her husband torturing her with two hacking knives. Yet, when the daughter speaks to her saying, "Poor mother, you walk in your sleep, as we have all done, but are you never to wake up?" the mother listens only for a split second. The next moment she has sunk back into blind self-adulation.

As always with Strindberg, good nourishment is identical with (maternal) love; feeding takes on ritual connotations, and all Strindberg's talk about the particulars of food is not a form of culinary pedantry but a metaphorical manner of speaking, referring to the giving or taking of life. The withholding of good food is therefore synonymous with murder. In *The Pelican*

Strindberg suggests that the dead husband was actually killed by the evil wife, just as the two children
(sickly enough to remind one of an Ibsen character like
Oswald Alving) are driven to self-annihilation through
the mother's methodical starving of them.

Although the concentration of evil seems greater in
The Pelican than in *The Ghost Sonata,* the ending of
the two plays offers certain parallels. After depicting the
pelican household in such dark colors that it implies, in
effect, a total rejection of life (culminating in the son's
bitter words: "My contempt for life, humanity, society,
and myself is so boundless I wouldn't raise my little
finger to go on living"), Strindberg's denunciation glides
into the seductive longing for death and innocence
that characterized the final scene of *The Ghost Sonata.*
In *The Pelican* the Toten-Insel motif takes the form of
a regression to childhood; as brother and sister are
consumed by fire, childhood memories pass by, taking
the form of a paradisical vision of a summer island
where the children and the father used to go down to
the steamer which brought people out to their summer
homes in the archipelago. Suddenly all evil is wiped
out and brother and sister face death in a mood of joyful
expectation.

In the summer of 1908 Strindberg moved into a new
modern house with electricity and elevator service,
which he gave the name "The Blue Tower." Here he
met a family with a number of small children and he
was again inspired to try his hand at plays in the fairy
tale genre. After a failure—*Abu Casem's Slippers*—he
wrote *The Black Glove* in which he combined the magic
of electric light with Christmas goblins and angels. He
gave the play the opus number 5 and included it among
the chamber plays. But its tone is lighter than in Opus
1 to 4, and Strindberg's handling of nonnaturalistic
elements is closer to naïvistic fantasy than to the gro-

tesqueness of the earlier chamber plays. The symbolic potential of the story about a nasty young wife whose daughter is kidnapped by fairy creatures is not pursued, and the work remains a trifle in Strindberg's production.

Beginning with *To Damascus*, a ruminating, quiet mood often breaks into Strindberg's dynamic dramatic material. Lyrical passages form restful pauses in *A Dreamplay* and *The Bridal Crown*. *Stormy Weather* and *The Burned House* have central characters who are largely meditative men, philosophizing about life. In 1909 Strindberg published a drama, *The Great Highway*, which is more or less composed of lyrical soliloquies that are designed to take the place of actual scene-painting.

Back in 1894 Strindberg had once written: "I have passed the noonday height of my life and now when I throw a glance at my past I often see myself in the guise of a hunter." It was in this role that he cast the main character in *The Great Highway*, the work which has been called Strindberg's literary testament. Like so many of Strindberg's works after the Inferno period, the autobiographical background of *The Great Highway* seems indisputable but so does the arrangement of the subject matter—what has been called "the codification of the experiential material," [7] a process that Strindberg himself describes in the prose fragment called *The Cloister*:

> By ruminating his experiences in this way he converted them imaginatively and by this procedure they became imprinted or fixed in his mind in such a way that he could have them at his disposal for future use as safely as means put in a bank.

The Great Highway opens with the Hunter climbing the Alps, seeking his soul in the land of eternal snow. Soon, however, he is tempted to return to earth and although he wants to remain an observer, he is drawn into a series of dramatic involvements. Joining company with the Wanderer, he witnesses an absurd dispute between two Millers and the ugly maneuvering of an ignorant, but influential Smith. Left alone after his companion enters a tavern, the Hunter meets a Japanese who tries to convince him of the beauty of suicide, and a murderer who has reared his daughter. The Tempter accosts him, promising him a rich life in the service of earthly masters. But in the end the Hunter departs, defending himself as "the solicitor of the only true One against the idol-worshippers" and asking God to bless him and all mankind.

The Hunter begins his circular wandering torn between a desire to settle his account on earth ("thou temptress that pulls me back") and a longing to find there a state of fulfillment ("the Land of Wishes"). His journey is designed as a *via dolorosa* between the seven stations of Golgotha; yet, his destiny is not that of a Christ-figure but as a representative of mankind. Although descending from the heights the Hunter lacks the metaphysical frame of reference of Indra's daughter in *A Dreamplay*. His next of kin, rather, is the Stranger in *To Damascus* (the similarity between the two plays extends to a conception of some of the secondary characters as projections of the protagonist's psyche). Through imagery of hindrance, aggression, and capturing, Strindberg makes the Hunter experience life on earth as a disillusioning and frustrating rat race. The Hunter has the same fighting spirit and displays the same unwillingness to accept a resigned view of life as the Stranger, but he has also absorbed some of the tired mellowness of the aging Strindberg.

When he returns to the mountains at the end of the play, the Hunter has severed all bonds with life on earth. His encounter with the suicidal Japanese has been the crucial episode. While the other characters have pointed out the futility of life to the Hunter, the Japanese has introduced the idea of a postexistence, referred to as "the summer vacation." It is the same expression as was used by the brother and sister at the end of *The Pelican*, and in both plays dying is associated with resurrection and conveyed to us by Christian sun symbolism.

The Hunter, having found life on earth "a lunatic asylum, a cage, a bow-net," rejects the world but not its creator. As he takes leave, he addresses a prayer to the divine power, in which he gives voice to Strindberg's lifelong and stubborn struggle with a dichotomous God whose "hard hand" conquers human beings with its "almighty goodness."

> *Here rests Ishmael, Hagar's son,*
> *who was once called Israel,*
> *because he had to fight with God,*
> *and did not cease until laid low,*
> *vanquished by His almighty goodness.*
> *Oh Eternal One! I shall not let go Thy hand,*
> *Thy hard hand until you have blessed me!*
>
> *Bless me, Your mankind,*
> *who suffers, suffers from Your gift of life!*
> *Me first who suffered most—*
> *who suffered most from the pain*
> *of not being what I wanted!*

The Great Highway has the quality of a choral song between two voices within one person. The drama was written to be read rather than staged, but the stylized decor is also a carry-over from Strindberg's experiences with the limited space of the Intimate Theatre, as well as the result of a renewed reaction against a minute, realistic stagecraft. Shakespeare became once more Strindberg's master, as he had been in his youth and again in the early 1900s when he sat down to plan his historical dramas, which will be discussed in chapter 7. Now it was Shakespeare as the supreme painter of words that fascinated him and led him to speak up for a renewed respect for dramatic speech: "The spoken word is the main thing and when Shakespeare's overly educated contemporaries could do without stage decor, we too can imagine to ourselves walls, barricades and trees. . . . For all is make-believe on the stage." [8]

7

Historical Dramas

In January 1899 Strindberg turned fifty—by tradition considered by most Swedes a festive and symbolic day in a man's life. Strindberg, who now lived in Lund, was celebrated as a creative writer by friends, poets, students, and journalists—a recognition that might have served as a major inducement for him to pursue, with renewed efforts, his work as a playwright. In the spring following his fiftieth birthday he completed the first in a series of dramas set in the Swedish past, *The Saga of the Folkungs.*

Several circumstances made Strindberg return to the historical drama, the genre in which he had made his debut as a playwright. *Master Olof* had been produced successfully in Stockholm in 1897, and one Swedish theater had chosen to honor Strindberg on his birthday with a staging of the play. In addition, the literary vogue both in Paris and Sweden was again directed toward the past, toward a world of myth and mystique. Strindberg also moved in historical-minded circles during his stay in Lund.

When Strindberg returned to historical writing, he retained his old habit of handling his sources very freely. Brushing aside the standard history books of his day, he resorted instead to a collection of legends of the past (*Sagohävder*) by Fryxell, Bäckström, and Afzelius, whose anecdotal approach to historical personages appealed to his sense of dramatic expediency and helped him overcome his occasional reluctance to alter old events, telescope historical time, and change biographical facts to reinforce a theme.

As in *Master Olof*, Strindberg's avowed aim in writing *The Saga of the Folkungs* and the other historical plays that appeared after his Inferno period was to depict the past "realistically," that is, to make it conform to his present view of life. This accounts for the philosophical gap existing between his early historical production and his plays after 1898. By the time he wrote *The Saga of the Folkungs*, Strindberg had long since rejected Buckle's evolutionary interpretation of history—history as materialistic progress—which had in part dictated his conception of *Master Olof*.

One might say, however, that the *Weltanschauung* Strindberg had now arrived at was more congenial to the genre of historical drama, for his view of human life as controlled by supernatural agents made him susceptible to the past as myth, as a symbolization of man's eternal fate. At the same time, Strindberg's religious standpoint had an associative anchoring in the past: his "powers" were in their nature and function not too different from ambiguous and fickle Fortune of the early Middle Ages; they were both awesome and providential, seemingly irrational but ultimately instruments of a divine and purposeful will. It was with this in mind that he wrote, in discussing his new dramas in his collection of *Open Letters to the Intimate Theatre*: "History is in broad outlines Providence's own composition." One of his basic motivations in writing the history plays was a desire to illustrate the working out from generation to generation of a harsh, retributive justice, using kings as figureheads, the struggle for the throne as the main theme, and the whole Swedish nation as the epic setting.

The formal conception behind Strindberg's plan was

no doubt influenced by a cyclic reading of Shakespeare's histories as these appeared in Hagberg's famous Swedish translation of 1847. Strindberg himself wrote in retrospect about the genesis of *The Saga of the Folkungs*:

> I made it my task, after my teacher Shakespeare . . . to let the historical be the background and shorten historical time according to the demands of the theater in order to avoid the undramatic form of chronicles and narratives. . . . My task was now to fuse into one person the bloody war of the Folkungs, which much resembles the War of the Roses in England.[1]

Originally, however, Strindberg's historical design seems to have been even more grandiose and expansive than his statement suggests. He planned a cycle of historical dramas that was to have covered almost seven hundred years of Swedish history and would have included many royal families. For a number of reasons his task was not completed, the most important being perhaps that his providential scheme was not always (as in Shakespeare) directly related to specified political motives. Politically, Strindberg held no views comparable to Shakespeare's Tudor myth and would not condone political expediency for the sake of maintaining a pseudoreligious concept of *de facto* kingship. Rather, he imposed his very personal vision of life on his characters so that they often appear strangely detached from the political action. There are exceptions, however. In *The Saga of the Folkungs* Strindberg depicts the King as symbolic figurehead only, and the controlling theme of retribution, demanding a largely passive victim, can therefore in part fuse with—and not, as so often in his later histories, be superimposed on—the political action.

The Saga of the Folkungs is the drama of King Magnus and begins when he is at the height of his powers.

But shortly after the spokesman of the slaves greets him as a "ruler of peace and savior" the divine powers turn against him: Russia attacks Sweden; Magnus's wife betrays him; the Queen Mother takes a former murderer of kings (Porse) as her lover; Magnus's son Erik schemes to force his father to abdicate; and a bishop, helped by the visionary nun Birgitta, plans to ban him; civil war threatens; and the plague is approaching the shores of the country. In the end Erik dies of the disease while Magnus, crushed, sinks down upon his son's body. In the distance one hears the sounds from the enemy's trumpets.

Like his master Shakespeare, Strindberg painted history on a broad canvas. The effect is a vivid and animated picture of a bustling world where the grotesque mingles with the pathetic, and where a whole age comes to life on the stage. Strindberg's conscious adaptation of Shakespeare's free composition allowed him maximum variety—widely spaced character groupings and wide changes of scenes, parallel actions, and multiple plots. In *The Saga of the Folkungs* Strindberg made bold use of three minor actions, the three contrasting love stories: The realistically depicted love-hatred of the Queen Mother and her lover; the intoxicating passion of Queen Blanche and Algotsson, a passion that fades away with approaching death; and the idyllic love of Erik and his sweetheart Beatrix.

But in spite of such multiplicity of erotic plot, *The Saga of the Folkungs* transmits a sense of firm dramatic control, achieved by relating the minor actions to the main theme of the play, King Magnus's expiation of an ancestral crime. Strindberg expresses this central motif not only in Magnus's personal destiny but in the very movement of the play—the strong ritualistic elements in the plague scene (inspired by Boccaccio), the choral singing, Birgitta's and the Maniac's prophesies.

King Magnus reigns at a time when only a forceful ruler could have preserved the crown against attack. But Magnus is a pious "weakling," more fit for a monastic life than for the ruling of a country. His mother Ingeborg reprimands him that he can never act and she complains to Porse: "My son has himself caused his fall . . . a ruler must be able to do the impossible." Strindberg suggests then that it is a serious shortcoming in a king ever to yield to despair. But the total effect of *The Saga of the Folkungs* conveys something more than a political issue about the demands of kingship. Magnus is defeated not only because he is weak but because God has chosen him as a *satisfactio vicaria*; the usurpation of the throne by the first Folkung is to be expiated through Magnus. On the literal level we have a king deposed by his rebellious people, but on the symbolic level we have a martyr of God used by his creator to fulfill the retributive purpose for which he was created. Thus Magnus transcends his role as the last of the Folkungs, suffering for an ancestral sin; through him his society is purged of its evil. Ingeborg and Porse are banished, Birgitta is penitent, and the play ends on a note of melancholy fulfillment. The metaphysical mood is further sustained in the plague scene in act 4, an image of a physically and spiritually diseased society, and in the appearances of the Madwoman fighting, like the Stranger in *To Damascus*, a battle with the Invisible One who tries to prevent her from making use of her clairvoyant powers. In such scenes local politics and disasters grow into a symbolic pattern of the human condition on earth, and the play achieves the power of a polyphonic apocalypse for the stage, with an epic scope rarely surpassed in Strindberg's dramatic production.

The vast perspective of *The Saga of the Folkungs* was not transmitted to Strindberg's next history play,

Gustav Vasa, even though the playwright retained the method of expanding the dramatic vision of reality to include court and tavern, king and country folk—in both instances a carry-over from *Master Olof* and Strindberg's readings of Shakespeare.

The play concentrates on two critical episodes during Gustav Vasa's reign, which in reality took place ten years apart but in Strindberg's drama are juxtaposed to each other in time: Gustav Vasa's inquisition in Dalarna and the Dacke uprising in Småland. Following Gustav Vasa's swift decision to execute two Dalecarlians and his decree to melt down the church bells for cannon balls, a rumor begins to circulate that the people of Dalarna will aid Dacke in his rebellion, assisted unwittingly by the city of Lübeck. Feeling threatened, Gustav Vasa makes himself ready to abdicate, confessing that he deserves his fate and has been justly punished by God. But the Dalecarlians have actually marched on the capital in order to offer the king their help and loyalty.

Like most of Strindberg's historical dramas to follow it, *Gustav Vasa* takes its title from the ruler, indicating an altered purpose in Strindberg's composition. He was no longer writing a religious saga but the life of a king. Instead of the panoramic spectacle of *The Saga of the Folkungs* we get in *Gustav Vasa*—in spite of its rapid movement and frequent shiftings of scene—a historical drama that is primarily a character study, centering around the king's dual conflict: the tension between him and his people and his private battle with God.

During the first half of the drama the title figure, though far from a religious symbol as was King Magnus in *The Saga of the Folkungs*, is nevertheless regarded by his people and his family as an ominous "duplicate" of the Eternal One, a concept which the king himself accepts. But as the drama proceeds, the king changes from a public symbol to a private man with family problems (his boozing son and successor, Prince Erik) and a guilty conscience. This metamorphosis is paralleled by a narrowing of the scope of the play as we move from the country into Stockholm, from Dalarna to the king's parlor. Gustav is still preoccupied with political problems and the threat of rebellion, but the focus is now to a large extent on his personal conflict. Here Strindberg makes an open and rather undramatic use of his providential philosophy but he restricts it to serve as personal motivation for Gustav. The result is that the earlier image of the king as a forceful and, for three entire acts, invisible ruler of his country now turns into a portrait of a monarch who substitutes action for a dependence upon divine protection.

Yet Gustav Vasa dominates the drama that bears his name. The supporting cast is grouped in Shakespearean manner to interrupt and reinforce the main action; the Lübeckian Jews Jacob and Herman Israel vary the royal father-son relationship, and Prince Erik and his boon companion Göran Persson (roughly corresponding to Prince Hal and Falstaff in *Henry IV*) are brought into the play to furnish a link with the already planned sequel *Erik XIV* but also throw the king's private worries into sharper focus.

Strindberg desired to see *Gustav Vasa* and *Erik XIV* as forming a group—the Vasa Saga. Their unity is, however, based on rather arbitrary devices: introduction of the same characters, references to historical data, and use of family genealogies. On the other hand, it is difficult to see any thematic connection between the two dramas or any motivated development in the central characters. Erik XIV merely changes from a madcap prince to a madcap king, while Göran Persson undergoes an inexplicable transformation from tavern cynic to sentimental and noble lover.

Erik XIV opens on the same castle terrace where *Gustav Vasa* ended. A messenger, Nils Sture, arrives with the word that Queen Elizabeth of England has turned down Erik's proposal of marriage. In rancor Erik turns against the Sture family and has two of its members murdered in prison. He then legalizes his liaison with his mistress Karin Månsdotter at a weird wedding banquet to which he has invited beggars and rascals. However, the feast comes to an end as the Dukes Charles and John arrive; the king is imprisoned but rivalry breaks out between his arresters. The play ends on a resigned, Swedenborgian note proclaiming that strife and suffering are integral parts of human life.

The Swedenborgian finale of *Erik XIV* is a remnant of the original conception of the play, in which Strindberg planned to make Erik's superstition a major theme. He was to have gone through a series of religious crises and finally end as an alchemist and black magician, abandoned and deposed by his people. But Strindberg, who had early identified Erik XIV with Hamlet,[2] became more and more absorbed in the neurotic aspects of Erik's personality. The drama grew into a study of "a characterless character," (i.e., a complex stage figure, as discussed in the preface to *Miss Julie*), and was presented on a much smaller scale than the earlier histories. It is no mere coincidence that *Erik XIV* opens, not with the Shakespearean throng and chorus of the barber scene in *The Saga of the Folkungs* or *Gustav Vasa*'s Dalecarlian inquisition, but with the furious Erik, who from his balcony throws nails, shoes, and flower pots on his councillor and his mistress. Throughout the entire play all the events, with the exception of Göran Persson's love story, are arranged primarily with a view to the effect they will have or the light they may throw on the king's personality. Yet the play does not give the impression of being conceived in great concen-

tration, but its structure partakes of some of the
shattered rhythm of King Erik's personal fate. The
action lacks the thematic stringency of *The Saga of the
Folkungs* and the dramatic firmness of *Gustav Vasa*,
but has instead the modern temper of an analytical
drama, coupled with a guilt motif of classic origin. Erik
is "doomed to certain crimes," like the heroes of old
Greek drama, although Strindberg tends to substitute
naturalistic determinism—the forces of heredity and
environment—for the absolute decrees of invisible gods.
In that sense *Erik XIV* marks a return to Strindberg's
pre-Inferno production.

In Strindberg's next historical drama, *Gustav Adolf*,
the toning down of the guilt problem, individual and
ancestral, which was already noticeable in *Erik XIV*,
led to an increased concentration on the objective-
historical background of the title figure. Gone in the
new play are both the philosophical mood of impending
doom and retribution, and the psychological close-up
of the monarch. Instead an atmosphere of tolerance and
religious syncretism pervades the tableaulike drama,
which has been called "the Thirty Years War in
memoriam." [3]

The play shows us the Protestant King Gustav Adolf
taking part in the war between Catholics and Protes-
tants in seventeenth-century Germany. We follow the
Swedish king from his landing on the island of Usedom,
through a country ravaged by vandalizing soldiers, to
the Protestant victory of Leipzig. After the fatal battle
of Lützen, the drama ends at the cathedral of Wittenberg where Gustav Adolf lies in state.

Gustav Adolf is an unwieldy play that would take
more than six hours to perform. Its scope, as well as its
lack of a unified dramatic action, indicates that Strindberg had too much disparate material at hand. He desired to give a panoramic view of the war and present its

social, religious, and psychological ramifications, but he failed to create a central character whose destiny was relevant to the mood and philosophical direction of the play. King Gustav Adolf is presented as both a defender of the Protestant faith and a spokesman of religious tolerance. His growing ambivalence and uncertainty about his own motives have dramatic potential, but Strindberg fails to pursue it—the king's humanistic, pacifist speeches have no bearing upon the course of his actions. Thus the strength of the play lies not in the portrait of the king but in individual scenes depicting the everyday horror of war, with beggars, fugitives, and wounded men spread over the devastated landscape. In the restless world of warring soldiers, ill omens seem to hide in the dense fog of the battlefield, suggesting powers at work stronger than the will of an individual king.

With the completion of *Gustav Adolf*—the play took him unusually long (six months) to finish—Strindberg lost interest in the historical drama for a while. When he returned to the genre in 1901, he had used the intervening fifteen months to write a number of contemporary dramas and folk plays. He had moved away from Shakespeare and now approached the melancholy mood drama of Maeterlinck, a development that left its mark on *Charles XII* (1901), even though Strindberg himself claimed that the play was a "drama of character and catastrophe, i.e., the last acts of a long story, and in this following somewhat the classical tragedies where everything has already happened." [4]

The play depicts the last phase in the life of King Charles XII. It opens as the king, after fifteen years of warring abroad, returns to the shores of Sweden. Here he encounters an impoverished country and a dissatisfied people. But he marches on Norway, and after an interruption of the doomsday atmosphere, during which the king discusses "the woman question" and quarrels with his sister Ulrika Eleonora, the play ends with the death of the monarch at Fredriksten's Castle.

Although basically a mood drama, *Charles XII* is the least inward-moving of Strindberg's historical plays; the playwright's conception of the "hero" king as "the berserk fighter, the idol of rascals" does not call for any soul analysis. Charles is a static character; he dies as he has lived, stubborn, morally inflexible, unscrupulous in his exploitation of others. When he speaks of himself, it is in self-defense rather than self-probing. Although Strindberg made Charles suffer from the same excessive pride as King Magnus and Gustav Vasa, he left out any trace of penitence or any sense of guilt in him; at the height of his devastating career Strindberg's Charles XII exclaims: "I have only defended myself, my country, my royal heritage!"

The dramatic conflict in *Charles XII* arises from an outer tension between the king and his grumbling people. Yet we never witness any real clashes between royal and popular wills. The reason for this is to be found in Strindberg's presentation of Charles. The king exists in a world apart from his people. He is almost always present, yet he is unattainable, or, as one character in the play remarks, "a dead man whose body walks about as a ghost."

Strindberg's intention in depicting Charles XII was to show us a man who has survived himself, whose idea of autocratic kingship is hopelessly out of tune with the democratic voice of the people. But Charles seems also to be conceived as a man existing beyond the borderlines of consciousness; he is actually an expressionistic character in an otherwise Naturalistic drama. The power of *Charles XII* lies, in fact, in this formal tension within the play.

Strindberg's next historical drama, *Engelbrekt*, is an

uninspired work where a melodramatic plot functions as a poor substitute for the title figure's lack of psychological plausability. But immediately after completing *Engelbrekt*, Strindberg began work on *Queen Christina*, a play about Gustav Adolf's daughter and successor who abdicated the crown to join the Catholic church. As might be expected, Strindberg's dramatization of one of Sweden's "earliest feminists" is both biased and provocative.

In his preface to *Miss Julie* Strindberg suggested that the illusory world of the stage suited the feminine psyche in particular, and many of Strindberg's women's portraits point, in fact, to an identification of the feminine and the theatrical. Women were, according to Strindberg, innately histrionic and chameleonlike, possessing something of the irresponsibility and capriciousness of a great actress. In this sense, his Christina stands as the very essence of womanhood, for she is a being in whom role-playing and self-revelation merge. She appears infantile, coquettish, heartless; yet these qualities are part of her true nature. Thus Queen Christina adapts herself to a new situation with the same intuitive cunning as Laura in *The Father*; she has brief moments of poignant insight but on the whole she is a creature of fateful ignorance.

Although Strindberg's Christina is not without depth, her constant role-playing keeps her from plunging into introspection and despair. She thereby sets the tone of the play; *Queen Christina* is the wittiest of Strindberg's historical dramas. Contemporary critics were in fact shocked, and experienced the play as a parody. Not mincing his words, one reviewer declared *Queen Christina* "a scampish, ignorant and inartistic work by a both intellectually and morally defective author." [5] Strindberg reacted with bitterness, claiming that his drama was among his finest works for the stage. Yet he could not dismiss the criticism, and when he planned a production of *Queen Christina* at his Intimate Theatre in 1908, he wrote to director August Falck: "Aim higher than I have done! Lift up the historic personages! And try to achieve a bit of grandeur and historical atmosphere. A little stiffness in the acting, conditioned by the costume; a little elegance (Molière) or else, to tell the truth, we fall into parody."

When Strindberg decided to write a play about Christina's male counterpart, Gustav III, he emphasized the elegant rococo style of the period. He had less difficulty with the historical authenticity of the royal portrait, for Gustav III was by tradition regarded as the great actor on the Swedish throne. Strindberg conceived the culture-conscious monarch as a talented artist, without depth and originality but with a good portion of charm and spirited audacity.

Strindberg's play begins just before the opening of the Swedish Riksdag (parliament) in 1789 when Gustav III staged a *coup d'étât* and, assisted by the commoners, expanded his royal powers. But Gustav III is an enlightened despot; Strindberg called him "a disciple of Frederic the Great, Joseph II, and Voltaire," and made him an entertaining but not a domineering character. In spite of political tensions, Gustav III is an easygoing man whose personality sets the tone for the entire play, which is free from Inferno problems and has the suspense and cleverness of a traditionally well-made play.

After *Gustav III* Strindberg persevered for yet a while in the genre of historical drama; he now began to choose foreign plots and settings in the hope of winning a greater success abroad than he had had in the Swedish theater. It was a bitter fact to him that in 1902 when he completed *Gustav III*, he had no less than six major dramas on his desk for which he could not find a Swedish producer. In the following year he wrote, therefore, an ambitious drama about Luther, aimed at a German public. But the play, titled *The Nightingale in Wittenberg*, was not performed in Strindberg's lifetime. It is a drama composed in the style of *Gustav Adolf*, with a series of historical vignettes and a large number of loosely-sketched characters. Strindberg had made extensive studies before writing the play, but as in *Gustav Adolf* his documentary ambitions outwitted his dramatic talent.

In the fall of 1903 Strindberg began planning a grandiose cycle of three five-act trilogies, based on world history. It was an old idea (from 1889) which now flared up again, but the plan soon evaporated, leaving behind only three minor plays about Moses, Christ, and Socrates. Again the documentary material dominated and the plays became mostly paraphrases of biblical and classical texts. It was obvious that Strindberg had drained his creative resources with regard to historical drama, at least for the time being. When, in 1903, *Gustav Adolf* became a fiasco in Berlin, the outer incentive to write history plays seemed gone as well.

Yet, five years later, at a time of great dramatic activity, Strindberg returned once more to the historical genre. The Royal Dramatic Theatre had expressed a desire to celebrate Strindberg's sixtieth birthday with a new play. Earlier in the year the playwright had experienced disappointment at the lukewarm reception of his chamber plays, which had turned out to be too shocking in mood and design for contemporary critics. Challenged to prove that he could still write good, entertaining drama, Strindberg wrote *The Last of the Knights*. The play, set in sixteenth-century Sweden and conventional in design, was completed in ten days. It did not prove, however, to inaugurate a successful comeback to the historical genre but seemed rather to be a faint reverberation of great figures and themes in Strindberg's earlier plays set in the Swedish past.

The play depicts the struggles of Regent Sten Sture

with the Danes and their supporters in Sweden, headed by the archbishop Gustav Trolle. The design is of an almost mechanical precision, setting up a psychological dichotomy between the mild and tolerant Sten Sture and the Machiavellian Trolle. The former is somewhat reminiscent of King Magnus in *The Saga of the Folkungs,* with whom he shares a fatal propensity for yielding to more unscrupulous men in power. He dwells so completely *sub specie aeternitatis* that he loses touch with the evil "trivialities" of life. Sture's detachment is related to the mood of the play, which is fatalistic and conveys a feeling that plotting and fighting are inevitable parts of human existence. In this respect, *The Last of the Knights* reveals its affinity with other works by the aging Strindberg; its element of resignation and longing for a spiritual refuge or hinterland aligns it with such dramas as *Easter, A Dreamplay, The Ghost Sonata,* and *The Great Highway.*

In his *Open Letters to the Intimate Theatre* Strindberg makes the statement: "To write a historical drama is somewhat like writing . . . a variation of a theme or a transcription of an already composed play." *The Regent* (1908) is conceived in that vein. It is a companion piece to *The Last of the Knights,* yet differs from it in mood and tempo as much as *Gustav Vasa* differs from *The Saga of the Folkungs.*

The central character in *The Regent* is Gustav Erikson, later Gustav Vasa. A bloodbath staged by the Danish tyrant and usurper King Christian has taken place. Christian's supporter Gustav Trolle dwells at the Royal Palace in Stockholm as Gustav Erikson, the liberator, approaches the city. Gustav Erikson has a series of confrontations with Trolle, Bishop Brask, and others, but in the end he can march into Stockholm and let himself be crowned king of Sweden.

The dramatic clashes, robust temper, and dynamic

speech of *The Regent* find no counterpart in the placid, almost anemic atmosphere of *The Last of the Knights*. The differences between the two plays crystallize around the central characters. While Sten Sture is an idealist, a courteous medieval knight who speaks in a slow and vacillating way, Gustav Erikson Vasa is a drastic and realistic politician whose language is rapid and cutting. The last of the knights emerges as a doomed, melancholy dreamer ("a sleep-walker"), but the future king of Sweden embodies swift action and a determination to fight an egotistical world on its own terms. The dramatic action of *The Regent* contains however, one unmotivated *volte face* after another and leaves the impression of incompleteness. The same is true of Strindberg's last historical drama, *Earl Birger of Bjälbo* (1909), although it is the most dynamic and best realized of his late history plays.

The title figure of *Earl Birger of Bjälbo* may have caught Strindberg's imagination as the founder of the Folkung Dynasty. Wanting to bring his historical production to a close, Strindberg perhaps felt that a play about the thirteenth-century regent and father of the first of the Folkungs would bring his history plays to a full circle.

The plot tells of how Earl Birger is tempted by his councillor Ivar Blue to seek the Swedish throne. The power-hungry earl tries to manipulate himself into a royal position by gradual elimination of contenders to the crown and by marriage to the Danish Princess Mechtild. He seems to succeed, but in the end his son Magnus "Barnlock" outwits him. Birger then withdraws in a resigned mood from his political activities.

Though impressive in its first notes, the play does not fulfill its early promises. The opening scene with the two chorus figures of the Watchman and the Fisherman talking about Earl Birger creates the same curiosity about the protagonist as did the beginning of *Gustav Vasa*. But the image of a mysterious, all-knowing ruler is never developed; instead Earl Birger soon disintegrates into a shallow manipulator, whose dichotomous moods—his drive for power and his penitential brooding—are not allowed to grow into an inner conflict.

There is in *Earl Birger of Bjälbo* a strange lack of rapport between Strindberg and his characters. He knows the rudiments of the trade and can give us vignettelike portraits of the supporting personages, but they remain shadows rather than fully rounded stage figures. It has been suggested that Strindberg's age may account for this. But his last history play does not give the impression of waning creative powers so much as an exhaustion of the genre itself. It is interesting to study Strindberg's account of the genesis of the work; excerpts from his *Open Letters to the Intimate Theatre* suggest to what an extent the historical drama had become sheer routine for him.

> When I wrote *Earl Birger of Bjälbo* I proceeded as usual. I read Starbäck's *History,* for I don't know that he has written any novel about Earl Birger. . . . To "create atmosphere" and move myself back to a distant time, I did as I usually do in writing my historical dramas: I read Walter Scott. . . . As usual in my historical dramas I have placed Swedish history within the frame of world history.

8

Poetry

Strindberg's prose works contain numerous references
to the art of poetry, almost all of them of a negative
nature. He early identified poetry with rhyme-making
and felt that to write verse one needed only a certain
technical competence but no real talent or inspiration
—as the poet Pedersen states in Strindberg's early one-
acter *In Rome*: "To put a rhyme at the end of the
line/ is a gift bestowed on everyone."

But verse-making to Strindberg was not only a skill of
little uniqueness; it was an objectionable occupation
since it tended to prettify life and make the poet escape
from ugly reality. In his attacks on poetry, Strindberg
saw himself both as a spokesman for truth in art, which
to him could only be expressed in straightforward realistic prose, and as a defender of the oppressed against
the upper classes, whose understrappers were the verse-
makers, falsifying reality and blinding the readers to the
misery of life. In an essay on Björnson, written in 1884,
Strindberg asks:

A well-liked poet, who has the right to say anything,
provided he says it nicely, isn't he like an actor, who,
dressed in polichinelle dress, steps forward to tell the
public with the greatest possible cautiousness that
there is a fire backstage? The public believes it to be

part of his role and receives him with applause and peals of laughter.

Strindberg's sarcastic or belittling remarks about poetry continued throughout his life. Yet with the exception of the period 1884–1901 he practiced the genre, using verse in his dramas or in separate volumes of poetry: *Poems (Dikter)* in 1883; *A Sleepwalker's Nights on Wakeful Days (Sömngångarnätter på vakna dagar)* in 1884; *Word Play and Minor Art (Ordalek och småkonst)* in 1905.

The reasons for Strindberg's lasting lack of enthusiasm for poetry—according to Harriet Bosse he seldom read verse and his library contained few volumes of poetry—should be set in relation to the literary climate during his formative years as a writer. Strindberg grew up and made his debut at a time when poetry in bound form was very much the genre in which an ambitious Swedish writer would prove his talents. The verse that Strindberg used in his early dramas, including his poetic edition of *Master Olof*, might be seen as a concession to the literary demands of his age. At the same time, he felt that poetry, at least in its current metric form and predominantly idyllic subject matter, was not his natural medium; the vehemence with which he often attacked poetry probably contained an element of self-condemnation at his own efforts in the field.

Strindberg had a definite objective with his first work of poetry, *Poems*. In one of his verses entitled "Singer," he maintains that truth must be ugly as long as beauty means artifice and prettification. Challenging traditional verse-making, he uses either an "unpolished" irregular form or employs a conventional verse interspersed with a number of prosaic or colloquial words. Yet it is an indication of Strindberg's poetic skill that *Poems* moves outside the orbit of the literary pamphlet. Today, when their shock effect is gone, many of Strindberg's poems from 1883 seem remarkable in their pregnant word choice and emotional intensity which usually strikes upon a relevant concrete image. And ironically enough Strindberg proves himself a skillful "rhymer" so that many of his poems achieve their impact from the poet's fusion of concise rhythm and rhyme (e.g., "The blasphemies of Loke"; "The Esplanade System").

Poems contains, among other things, a fragment entitled "Sleepwalker Nights, the First Night," which a year later was to form the first part of a collection of poetry consisting of a cycle of five "Sleepwalker Nights." In unrhymed couplets—a verse form he had used in the poetic version of *Master Olof*—Strindberg depicts a philosophical journey back in time. The frame (except for the first poem) consists of a series of French settings but the central motif of the entire collection revolves around the poet's imagined returns to Sweden and to places considered important for his development—to the church where he was confirmed but which he now denounces; to the National Museum in Stockholm, where he proclaims the uselessness of art and the futility that lies in man's worship of beauty; to the Royal Library in Stockholm where he experiences a Swiftian battle of books and arrives at the conclusion that in the future, libraries will be filled with newspaper articles relating factual events rather than books disputing unsolvable problems or depicting reality in false colors; and finally to the Swedish countryside with its "flowering reeds," "white birch trees," "strawberry patches and shoals of perch."

Sleepwalker Nights contains a denunciation of the self-sufficiency, specialization, and isolation of modern scientists, and advocates a return to nature—"live free and proud in your stark nature." Yet the poem does not transmit much of the optimism of this Rousseau-inspired philosophy. Rather, it ends with a vision of the possible annihilation of mankind and of the world.

This apocalyptic conclusion runs parallel to a pessimistic *Weltanschauung* derived from the German philosophers Hartmann and Schopenhauer, which had inspired Strindberg earlier in the verse edition of *Master Olof* and in the diary of Olof Montanus in *The Red Room*. Yet, juxtaposed to this glum vision of the future, we find a view reminiscent of that of Arvid Falk in the novel from 1879; seemingly shunning the attitude of the defeatist, Strindberg exhorts man to become *l'homme engagé*, an individual working for the welfare of others in the knowledge that his own life is ordinary rather than unique and exceptional.

Such advocacy of a life of social commitment may have been inspired by the writings of Björnstierne Björnson and Jonas Lie, the two Norwegian realists whom Strindberg had met in Paris and to whom he dedicated *Sleepwalker Nights*. Ironically enough, his attempt to set up an optimistic faith in communal progress and welfare against his own reckonings with the past and his skepticism with the present and the future was pretty much in vain. Björnson's reception of Strindberg's work was quite tepid, no doubt because he missed in it the voice of the whole-hearted utilitarian. But for posterity *Sleepwalker Nights* has become a fascinating poem precisely because of its author's philosophical ambivalence. It derives much of its power from Strindberg's inner duelling between a matter-of-fact concept of the useful individual in a world without fanciful illusions and an ironic reproach of the level-headed realist who believes fully in man's accomplishments but forgets the presence of a Creator—who "believes in the shoe but denies the shoemaker." As Henry Olson has stated in his analysis of Strindberg's cycle, *Sleepwalker Nights* "represents a monument over the two contending, basic tendencies in Strindberg's temperament—the need to doubt and the need to believe." [1]

It took more than twenty years before Strindberg published another volume of poetry, but his urge to question the value of polished verse was as great in 1905 as in 1883. In fact, a few years before the appearance of *Word Play and Minor Art* Strindberg stated in a letter to Schering: "A work of art should be a little careless, imperfect like a product of nature where not a crystal is without its faults, not a plant without a defective leaf."

The unpretentious and belittling title of *Word Play and Minor Art* indicates that Strindberg still tended to question the *raison d'être* of poetry. Yet his point of departure in the early 1900s was radically different from his Naturalistic prose position in 1882–83. When he wrote *Word Play* he had behind him a number of dramas in which lyrical sections were dominant, most notably *The Bridal Crown, Swanwhite,* and *A Dreamplay.* Several of the poems in *Word Play,* for instance "Trinity Night" and "The Dutchman," were in fact planned as verse dramas. Most of them have also a distinct dramatic composition, depicting an evolution or a movement rather than a condition or state of mind. In this respect Strindberg's verse differed most notably from the poetry of his contemporaries.

The 1890s are usually considered to have brought a lyrical renaissance to Swedish literature, with a poetry that tended toward nature lyricism and aestheticism. In the program set forth in the early nineties by the poets Heidenstam and Levertin, the key concepts were beauty (as opposed to "truth"), imagination (as opposed to rational exactness), romantic subject matter (as opposed to realistic motifs). But although Strindberg's poems of 1882 might epitomize what Heidenstam and Levertin objected to in poetry, his *Sleepwalker Nights* of 1883 already contained many of the elements that the so-called "pepita school" manifesto called for: nostalgic mood and idyllic scene-painting juxtaposed with occasional colloquialisms in style. *Word Play*, on the other hand, transcended—in its dependence upon dream and fantasy and its use of visionary symbolism—the Swedish poetry of its day and actually pointed beyond Strindberg's own lifetime toward surrealistic movements of a later period.

The poetic motifs in *Word Play* span many areas but the element of satire, rather important in the poems of the eighties, is now on the wane. Didacticism still breaks through in poems like "Rosa mystica" and "The Laws of Creation." Strindberg tries his hand at poetry of an almost epic and narrative scope. An example is "City Journey," written in iambic verse (hexameter), which paints the idyllic landscape around Stockholm in precise, harmonic strokes. In other poems Strindberg cultivates the realistic vignette, occasionally expanding it into amusing tableau of contemporary living. But it is the experience of the Inferno crisis that leaves its most distinct marks on *Word Play*. It is noticeable in the numerous allusions to magic and occult phenomena and in the melancholy, dreamlike mood that permeates such central poems as "Chrysaetos" and "I Dreamt"— both of them part of "Trinity Night." In hectic, hallucinatory passages "Chrysaetos" depicts a man's search for a dead woman, while "I Dreamt" portrays a marriage reminiscent of the Lawyer's and Agnes's in A *Dreamplay*, except that now there is no release, only an agonizing repetition of the same evil dream:

> *Then I cried loud: "Is there no end,*
> *Is there no end to this hell?"*
> *There was no end; and every night brings back the*
>   *dream*
> *That has become like my second life.*

9

Melancholia and Militancy
From *Alone* to *Black Banners*

It is hardly surprising that Strindberg decided, in the spring of 1902 to return to fiction and poetry, for on the whole he had failed to arouse an interest among theater producers in his dramas written after 1898. But a letter written a few years later reveals that he still considered drama his actual genre: "The secret of all my tales, short stories, fairy tales, is that they are dramas. When the theaters were closed to me for long periods of time, I got the idea of writing my dramas in epic form—for future use."[1]

Fairhaven and Foulstrand, the first new work of fiction to appear, was a collection of short stories, many of which have an anchoring in the world of *A Dreamplay* and *The Ghost Sonata*. Of greater novelty is *Alone*, an autobiographical novella published in 1903. Strindberg gives an account of his life as an artist after his separation from Harriet Bosse. The tone of *Alone* is resigned and melancholy; it is the work of a man who seems to have accepted the life of a recluse. Although sociable by nature, Strindberg felt it to be increasingly difficult to find congenial people who shared his interests and ideas; his irritability was considerable, as he was well aware: "Since my thoughts do not team up with anybody else's, I become hurt by almost anything that's said and I can often feel an innocent word like an insult." Yet *Alone* also reveals Strindberg's maintained curiosity about other people, though with a writer's distance firmly established between him and the outside world. Rather than close contact he craves quick impressions and fragmentary pieces of information about others; these nourish his imagination and help him create destinies for the people he meets during his daily morning walks. He does his real living while sitting alone at his writing desk:

> The strength I picked up outside . . . now serves my different aims. . . . I crawl out of my own skin and speak out of the mouth of children, women, and old men; I am king and beggar, I am a man of high station, a tyrant and the most despised of all, the oppressed hater of tyrants; I possess all opinions and subscribe to all religions; I live in all ages and I myself have ceased to be. This is a state that fills me with indescribable happiness.

The creative autonomy and meditative distance that characterize *Alone* also determine the mood of *Fairy Tales* (*Sagor*), published in the same year and probably inspired by the birth of Strindberg's daughter Ann-Mari in 1902. His literary model was supposed to be Hans Christian Andersen, but only a few of the thirteen tales in the collection seem to share Andersen's melancholy naïvete and his ability to surround everyday objects with an aura of magic. Some of Strindberg's fairy tales are more like brief, realistic sketches, among them the well-known "Half a Sheet of Paper," which combines meticulous milieu painting with a mood of nostalgia reminiscent of *Alone*. Another of the more successful tales, "The Tribulations of the Lighthouse Keeper," transcends the world of realism but has more in common with Poe's ghost stories than with Andersen's fairy tales.

In *Alone* Strindberg presented himself as the detached

artist. In *Fairy Tales* he tried to withdraw behind the mask of an anonymous storyteller. Soon afterward, however, he appeared in his old militant role of social critic; he published a novel, *Gothic Rooms*, which was meant to be a parallel and a continuation of *The Red Room*, written exactly twenty-five years earlier (Strindberg easily fell under the spell of numbers). The critics seized upon the opportunity to compare the two works and found *Gothic Rooms* lacking in the satirical vitality and dynamic characterization of *The Red Room*.

The title refers to the same, now renamed locale as in the earlier novel, and the people from *The Red Room* appear again, with the exception of Arvid Falk who is dead. The central role is played by Borg, now an aged medical doctor, and by his relatives. No one in the novel is conceived as a well-rounded character, but all emerge as personifications of Strindberg's social and private thoughts. The mood is negative and the milieus depicted are either gloomy or degenerate. The archipelago is no longer a peaceful summer retreat but is seen in late autumn and winter and is inhabited by people who are by and large lonely failures. Nature possesses no restorative power. Life in Stockholm is a caricature of decadence and offers a much more bitter view of society than the melancholy *mal de vivre* present in Swedish literature at the time. In fact, underneath the social criticism one senses a welling-forth of personal antipathy for all physical aspects of life. In the mouth of his intellectual spokesman Count Max, Strindberg's misanthropy reaches Swiftian proportions: "You know, once at the swimming school I saw the white-reddish human bodies and was struck by their likeness, not to apes but to young swine, which are also rosy red and hairless."

Gothic Rooms was not well received and Strindberg's acerbity grew worse. Next he wanted to settle his account with the literary world; the result was *Black*

Banners, read and received as a tasteless diatribe by a vengeful old man. Not until recently have Strindberg scholars begun to reevaluate the work, which should more correctly be regarded as a novel in the tradition of *The Red Room* but possessing a good deal of the quality of counterfeit confession that characterized A *Madman's Defense*.

Black Banners has the subtitle "moral tales from the turn of the century." Strindberg's purpose was twofold: he wished to reveal the corruption that existed among writers and newspapermen, but he also set out to advocate a possible road to salvation. The novel moves accordingly between two diametrically opposed milieus, the home of "little Zachris" and his wife Jenny, and the monastery on Sikla Island outside of Stockholm. The first nine chapters deal, in a satirical tone reminiscent of *The Red Room*, with the infernal world of "black banners" where a group of hypocrites do their best to hurt each other, illustrating the Swedenborgian thesis that "hell is not a place but a state of mind." The central passage in this early part of the novel is the nightmarish dinner at Professor Stenkål's, another example of a Strindbergian ghost supper. But Zachris's house, too, reveals an atmosphere of falsehood and abuse. A visitor easily discovers the phoniness of the home where "a gull was called a sea eagle, two bookshelves were called a library; a plaster bust of the grinning Voltaire was called a work of art." Zachris himself is a second-rate artist driven by his ambition and lack of imagination to use the sufferings of his wife as a basis for his writing.

From the tenth chapter on, every other chapter is devoted to the ethereal, dematerialized, and passionless world of Count Max and the monastery. The diatribe on "a rotten era" now alternates with religious didacticism, as Strindberg proceeds to depict the monastery as a refuge for those who have saved themselves from the evil influence of society. Life in the monastery offers no alternative to living; it is a rejection of life. In fact, several details in Strindberg's description of the religious asylum on Sikla Island indicate that he meant the monastery to be the symbolic abode of the "dead," of those who have withdrawn from life altogether.[2]

The monastery is designed for those who are meek and truly repentant. Some people, however, are totally beyond rescue, and Zachris is apparently one of them. He is described by others as the epitome of evil, a somewhat surprising indictment since the crimes he commits seem hardly of a satanic nature. But to Strindberg, Zachris represents vileness incarnate because he is a vampire, a nonentity who exists only by parasiting on others. Thus Zachris is likened to a thief who steals from the good, a cannibal who eats people.

Jenny, Zachris's wife, seems at first his fitting companion. A Strindbergian fury, she brings up the children to torture their father. She detests her husband as a sexual partner and later—after a religious conversion— as a symbol of wickedness. She shows that Zachris is utterly damned because he does not even long for peace. In spite of certain occult signs—his unfriendly reception at a restaurant, his horror at returning to an empty home on Christmas Eve—Zachris is said to be "too stupid" to realize the warnings sent him by the Eternal One. He seems, in fact, to be designed as a Swedenborgian spirit, destined to haunt the earth ("hell"). As such his impact is strong; when Count Max talks about him, the air seems poisoned. It is only by the "magic" of Beethoven's ethereal music that Zachris's evil presence can be made to disappear from the room.

In an attempt to bridge the gulf between Zachris's world and that of the monastery, Strindberg introduces the young writer Falkenström, in many ways a reincarnation of Falk in *The Red Room*. His fate illustrates Strindberg's belief (taken from Swedenborg) that the individual provokes his own destiny in society. As long as he is aggressive and vengeful, Falkenström is victimized, while his eventual retirement to Sikla Island eliminates all hostile moves against him.

The fate of both Jenny and Falkenström might seem to indicate that contemplative withdrawal is the answer to the destructive challenge of society. Strindberg suggests, however, another solution. Through the character of Smartman, a member of the world of shady morals who goes through a regeneration of spirit, he presents, at the end of *Black Banners,* a view of life that calls for personal integrity and self-adjustment rather than strict adherence to a religious or contemplative life. It reveals once more Strindberg's need as an artist to remain aloof from any dogmas and parties but also his deep-rooted admiration for the dutiful bourgeois life:

> If you are a poet or artist, you shall live outside of social classes, outside of parties, and yet preserve the interests of your colleagues, seeking justice, following your genius. As a poet you have a right to play with ideas, experiment with points of view but without committing yourself to any, for freedom is the poet's air of life. . . . If you are a bourgeois, then be so thoroughly. . . . Remain in your class and you will be something whole; and be careful of dilettantism.

It took Strindberg three years to find a publisher for *Black Banners,* and when the book finally appeared on the market it caused an immediate scandal not unlike that which occurred to Dante after the publication of his *Divine Comedy*. In both cases the reading public recognized well-known people from their own society as models for the tormentors and victims inhabiting the infernal world created by the respective authors. In Strindberg's case, the readers were also shocked by the intensity of the hatred and by a psychological approach that emphasized the grotesque and sadistic in human nature.

The characters in *Black Banners* belong to the world of the stark fairy tale; they have the quality of archetypes, and today it is difficult to imagine how anyone in Strindberg's time could identify them with real-life persons. No doubt Nathan Söderblom, archbishop of Sweden and a personal friend of Strindberg, was right when he pointed out that "when the personal key has been lost with time, the demonic power of the fictional characters will remain, a power which no doubt stems from someone other than the smaller, nicer people who now recognize themselves." [3]

Strindberg began, early in his career, to jot down daily episodes and thoughts with the idea in mind that they might be of use as literary material. From the time of the Inferno experience to the end of his life, he kept a diary where he noted especially the relationship between external events and inner experience. Some of this material became the basis for *Inferno* and *Legends*; some was only recently published under the title of *The Occult Diary*. After the appearance of *Black Banners* Strindberg put together a selection of notes which became the first volume of *A Blue Book*; he intended it as "a commentary to *Black Banners*." Several volumes were published later, the last one posthumously.

A Blue Book can actually be approached as an explicatory companion piece to most of Strindberg's works after the Inferno period. It contains discussions of his syncretist religion but alludes also to such themes in his dramas as the *Doppelgänger*, sleepwalker, and vampire motifs. He relates his idea of human parasites to Cinnober, the vampire in the works of E. T. A. Hoffman. Strindberg—more suggestively—calls the type "the sticky one":

> There are sticky people, insufficient, empty people who cannot live on their own root but must sit upon another's branch, like the mistletoe, which is very sticky so that one can make glue out of it. It is the sticky one who writes the long letters about nothing, offers services to be able to put someone in debt, becomes enraged if you don't write eight pages to him about nothing. . . . When he is alone some time in the summer, he withers and loses weight but he is almost never alone, for he always rents to be near you or your friends.

A *Blue Book* should not, however, be regarded merely as a reference work for students of Strindberg's late dramas and novels. Rinman and Brandell have already pointed out A *Blue Book*'s importance as an independent work; in it Strindberg reveals the intellectual span, the nervous tension and emotional ambivalence that combined to make him a poor scientist but an ingenious and highly dramatic writer. For a portrait of Strindberg, A *Blue Book* is almost as valuable as *The Son of a Servant*, even though its nonliterary sections are likely to chase away many a reader.

In the spring of 1906 Strindberg wrote his last two works of fiction, *Taklagsöl* (*The Roofing Party*) and *Syndabocken* (*The Scapegoat*). *The Roofing Party* is to a large extent a dramatic monologue by a dying man who has just undergone an operation and become talkative under the influence of morphine. His speech, rambling from lyrical reminiscences to feverish accusations heightened to the point of nightmarish visions, leads the thought to such chamber plays as *The Ghost*

Sonata and *The Pelican,* with their oscillation between
a grotesque experiencing of life and a nostalgic longing
for peace.

The title of the book refers to a newly built house that
the sick man, a conservationist, can see from his
window. His feverish mind concentrates more and
more upon "the green eye" which he sees in the apartment of an enemy who has moved into the new building. The novella revolves in part around the conservationist's attempt to come to terms with "the green
eye," with life itself.

Reality is cruel and hostile to the dying man. Life is
endurable and sweet only by one's withdrawal from
human company. The conservationist is happy when
he can live with imaginary people, "with my dear
shadows." Such a life of fantasy prepares him for death,
for a time when he shall turn his "back on it all, become independent, unreachable."

The Roofing Party belongs to the same type of
modernistic novellas as Hamsun's *Hunger*; works which,
though descriptions of a physical condition, expand into
a mental vision of life, with the authors using a technique that was later to be called stream-of-consciousness.
Strindberg's story is perhaps less successful than
Hamsun's in fusing the narrative sequences with the
"ravings" of the speaker; nevertheless it seems of considerable historical significance.

The Scapegoat was originally planned as a fragment
of *The Roofing Party.* It is a realistic story of great re-
straint that grows into a tale of psychological complexity.
In the center of action stands Libotz, a lawyer, who has
opened practice in a small Swedish town. Though a
man of integrity and humility, he is distrusted and ridiculed by the townspeople. A visit from his alcoholic
father ruins his reputation. A brief engagement to a
waitress ends abruptly with Libotz as the jilted lover.

His discovery of his clerk's embezzlement of funds is turned against him and he is fined for slander. Although later freed in the circuit court, Libotz is evicted from his lodging and, at the end, leaves town.

Though a *pharmakos*, a sacrificial, alienated man, Libotz gives the impression of a strong, self-sufficient creature. His brief love affair brings this out. When he and his fiancée go for walks, Libotz cuts a comic figure; he simply cannot communicate with the girl; his desperate attempts to do do belong to the most humorous passages that Strindberg wrote. But when the girl finds solace with the sheriff while Libotz falls asleep, Strindberg succeeds in depicting Libotz's withdrawal in a resigned, dignified mood. The same ambiguity is inherent in the book's ending. The lawyer is virtually destroyed, yet he leaves town with the composure of a man who cannot really be touched by the injustices of his fellowmen. He illustrates that independence of spirit which is characteristic of the aging Strindberg.

Although Libotz is the crucial character in *The Scapegoat*, Strindberg's psychological interest centers on a constellation of three men, the lawyer, the innkeeper (Askanius), and the sheriff (Tjärne). Through their reciprocal relations Strindberg reveals two of his essential ideas about the human psyche: that man is a chameleon with many selves, and that evil in man is parasitical, expressing itself in psychic murder.

Askanius is on the surface a humble, anonymous, and noncommittal person, but he has little of Libotz's kindness or peace of mind. Beneath his skin he harbors the frustrations of a small-town entrepreneur. Under the influence of liquor he can become seized with delusions of grandeur. An arrogant, Napoleonic side of his nature emerges in the ambitious restaurant project he conceives, the aim of which is to make him number one among business people in town. Performing "a series of Proteus performances" Askanius tries desperately to impress his surroundings.

But the real villian in *The Scapegoat* is not Askanius but Tjärne. The sheriff is a kin of Zachris in *Black Banners*, a nonentity who feeds on others. Libotz and Askanius both enable the sheriff to stay alive in town. From the lawyer, Tjärne steals reputation and fiancée; from Askanius he extracts confidence and succeeds in coming out of the whole situation with a good-conduct mark.

Strindberg's later prose works have never attained the same popular status as *The Red Room* and his short stories. Recently, however, Strindberg scholars have begun to pay attention to such novels as *A Madman's Defense*, *Black Banners*, *The Scapegoat*, and *Alone*, and these works are no longer regarded simply as fictionalized confessions or acts of revenge. It has been shown that they maintain an ironic distance between author and narrator, at the same time as they join company with the inward-directed novels of our century leading up to the works of Proust, Kafka, Joyce, and Faulkner.

10

The End and Its Aftermath

In the last years of his life Strindberg became involved once more in the social and political discussions of his time. Among the last things he published before he died of cancer of the stomach in the spring of 1912—an illness that seems almost psychosomatic in view of his fastidious and symbolic preoccupation with food—was a series of newspaper articles, the first of which was directed against the Swedish cult of Charles XII. The discussion which lasted for almost two years (1910–12) and involved more than one hundred articles by Strindberg became generally known as the "Strindberg Feud." Its original subject of debate soon expanded to include all aspects of Sweden's social, political, and literary life. Strindberg wrote about such diverse topics as the Swedish Academy, monarchy versus republic, syncretist religion, the Olympic Games, the new military spirit, the contemporary theater. The undaunted spirit behind these newspaper writings tempted the young radicals of the time to adopt Strindberg as their master, even though his socialist leanings were rooted in Rousseau rather than in Marx.

As a result of the "Strindberg Feud," the Swedish public went back to their early impression of Strindberg as a social critic. His popularity came to rest on his reputation as a political firebrand, not as a creator of a new drama. To most of his Swedish contemporaries it seemed, in fact, that as a creative writer Strindberg no longer communicated with the world after his Inferno experience. *To Damascus, A Dreamplay,* and the chamber plays, which are now recognized as perhaps Strindberg's greatest contribution to the modern theater, were received with much scepticism and reservation in their own time, and the late fictional works were often dismissed as vicious diatribes on hated competitors and enemies. John Landkvist, the editor of Strindberg's collected works, once remarked that those for whom *The Red Room* had been a tremendous literary event could never quite overcome their disappointment at the author of *To Damascus, A Dreamplay, The Ghost Sonata,* and *Black Banners.*[1]

There is an indication that today's generation of politically conscious Swedes is about to reassess Strindberg's role as a spokesman for social anomalies. Nonliterary critics like Jan Myrdal, although not looking upon Strindberg as a political rebel, share an ideological interest in him with his earliest supporters. Yet now, sixty years after his death, it seems indisputable that it is as a *literary artist* that Strindberg is an overshadowing giant. Certainly no Swedish writer before or after him has quite combined his creative vigor, linguistic versatility, or acute sense of drama with his encompassing vision of a transitional cultural epoch and his metaphysical probing. And no one has quite matched the emotional intensity of his works; in that respect Strindberg's own words have remained true—"I do not have the greatest intellect, but the fire; my fire is the greatest in Sweden."[2]

Strindberg's literary *oeuvre* seems to describe both a thematic cycle and a formal evolution. In this dichotomy lies perhaps the answer to his greatness. In order to understand his contribution to modern literature it is

first important to recognize that Strindberg's idiosyncra-
cies—his ambivalence toward women, his class consciousness, his belief in racial selection (as discussed in
his collection of essays *Vivisektioner*), even his religious
fluctuations—were tied to a permanent, emotional an-
choring-ground and tended to furnish his works with a
number of recurrent themes. Yet it would be too simple to say that Strindberg was content to present motifs
of sexual incompatability or social and religious conflicts
as refractions from a private mirror. The German and
early English translations of *Plaidoyer d'un fou* as
"Confessions of a Fool" is an example of an agelong
tendency to treat Strindberg as a writer for whom cre-
ativity became synonymous with momentary therapy
and private catharsis. Several Freudian studies attest
to this approach as being pretty much the standard one
to Strindberg. The result has been not only the usual
psychoanalytical debunking of the artist but also an ob-
scuring of the fact that Strindberg incorporated far more
of the *Zeigeist* into his works than he is given credit
for. Like most artists Strindberg was of course selective
in his use of current ideas, and he tended to look to the
outside intellectual world for generic support of his own
subjective thoughts. The eclectic but absolute way with
which he would embrace an essay or a book—for instance works by Lombroso, Lafargue, Rousseau, Darwin,
and Nietzsche—indicates an intense search for intellectualized confirmations of personal feelings rather than
an interest in ideas qua ideas.

Few literary men, however, break new philosophical
ground, as Strindberg himself indicates in his preface to
Miss Julie: "I see the playwright as a lay preacher ped-
dling the ideas of his time in popular form. . . .I have
not tried to do anything new, for this cannot be done,
but only to modernize the form. . . . To this end I
have chosen . . . themes which . . . have been and
will be of lasting interest."

In our often misconstrued notion that creative writers are philosophical innovators, we might perhaps keep in mind that Rousseau preceded the romantics; that Hegelian aesthetics was responsible for the emphasis on the idea in Hebbel's middle-class drama; that Kierkegaard inspired such different and chronologically separated writers as Ibsen and Kafka; that the existentialists of the forties helped shape the absurdist theater, but not until a decade later. Literary artists thus tend to work in the aftermath of great new ideas. But in so doing they make public what until then has only been limited intellectual property and, possibly, an inarticulate feel of the times. (It seems to me far more likely that, within a few decades, we shall produce writers who will succeed in creating the literary art of the space age and of the age of global revolution and social reorientation than that we will enter forever McLuhan's antiliterary universe.)

For artists to be great it is not enough that they be the recorders and disseminators of current ideas. Through their very artistic expression and formal presentation they must seem either to reach a kind of perfection, such as Shakespeare's and Ibsen's, which later generations of writers may try to emulate; or they must initiate new formal trends to be pursued and completed by their successors. It is to this second category of writters that Strindberg belongs.

Ingmar Bergman, in a very moving essay, has compared his work for the cinema to the construction of the great cathedral of Chartres, which was not the work of a single master architect but the composite result of efforts undertaken by scores, maybe hundreds of people. Strindberg's relationship to the modern theater might be seen in a similar way. He laid the basis of our contemporary stage in such plays as *A Dreamplay*, *The Dance of Death*, *The Ghost Sonata*, and *The Great Highway*. He did not complete the new structure as did Ibsen in terms of middle-class tragedy, but he indicated what the final building might look like and then left it to later playwrights to carry on the work. Thus Strindberg must be given credit for anticipating that erosion in the conflicts of ideology and character, and that fusion of stylized imagery, metaphysical mood, and petrified tension which are characteristic features in so much of today's theater.

Though Ibsen revolutionized bourgeois tragedy, he usually ordered his vision around a dramatic conflict capable of thematic progression and containing at least an implication of a different, less catastrophic solution. Strindberg's best-known dramas, on the other hand, seem to revolve around a fixed situation rather than a problem in human cohabitation. The characters have not really created the situation; it is created for them by life itself—in the Naturalistic plays by forces of heredity and environment but also and above all by the inborn warfare between male and female; in the post-Inferno dramas by "the powers"—those mystical forces that enabled Strindberg to transfer an amoral and biologically rooted struggle to a moral and metaphysical plane.

In his attempt to find objective validity for his personal vision, Strindberg often reduced his characters to essences rather than persons. These abstracted characters are beings who often live lives of circular motion and spend their time taunting each other in desperate relationships based on agonized mutual dependence, from which only death can rescue them. Their human condition is claustrophobic and the world they know a closed-in cage, which is reflected also in the prisonlike imagery and stage symbols that prevail in Strindberg's major dramas both before and after the Inferno experience; from the straitjacket in *The Father* and the caged bird in *Miss Julie*, to Kristin's pasted-up windows in *A Dreamplay*, the enclosing death screen and confining closet in *The Ghost Sonata*, and the

Hunter's experiencing of life as a treadmill, a trap, and a fishnet in *The Great Highway*.

Such diverse playwrights as Eugene O'Neill and Tennessee Williams on one hand, and Pinter, Ionesco, Albee, and Peter Weiss on the other have acknowledged their indebtedness to Strindberg. His impact can be felt in the harrowing exposures of marital hell in *Long Day's Journey into Night* and *Who's Afraid of Virginia Woolf?* In the plays of Beckett, Ionesco, and Pinter one senses Strindberg's spirit in the visual rather than philosophical projection of life as enclosure and confinement; in the use of the stage as a self-contained universe; in the centering on people going through mechanical, repetitious motions, questioning their suffering, yet only vaguely aware of their metaphysical agony; and in the view of existence as a waiting for release from suffering or as a place where the weak seem chained and trampled on by the ruthless.

One wonders why Strindberg continues to be largely ignored, except possibly for a passing tribute to *A Dreamplay*, by students of drama. Many have repudiated Strindberg's works because these seldom seem to offer any moral alternatives or situations capable of meaningful change, but are based rather rigidly on biological and/or metaphysical determinism. His elemental approach to character produces at times dramas with an almost unbearable sense of emotional suffering, thus inviting charges against their author for being too sick or too pessimistic. Yet, although Strindberg's vision of life appears indeed dreary (except when he is tempted to sentimentalize it by transforming it into either saccharine nostalgia or a Buddhistic cloud cuckooland), he gave that vision a dramatic form so startling and challenging that he opened up new avenues for modern drama which are only now being fully explored and recognized by other playwrights.

Notes

1 – A Note on Strindberg

1. Robert Brustein, *The Theatre of Revolt* (Boston: Little, Brown & Co., 1964), p. 95.

2 – Master Olof

1. Carl Reinhold Smedmark, "När Strindberg blev dramatiker," *Meddelanden från Strindbergssällskapet*, 30–31 (May, 1962), 16–17.

2. Martin Lamm, *August Strindberg* (Stockholm: Aldus, 1948), p. 37.

3 – From the Red Room to On the Seaboard

1. Quoted in Torsten Eklund, "Strindberg–det moderna genombrottets man i svensk litteratur," *Studiekamraten*, 19, No. 8–9 (1937), 124.

2. Göran Printz-Påhlson, "Krukan och bitarna," *BLM*, 33, No. 10 (1964), 750.

3. Cf. Göran Printz-Påhlson, "Krukan och bitarna," *BLM*, 34, No. 1 (1965), 20.

4. Göran Lindblad, *August Strindberg som berättare* (Stockholm: Norstedt, 1924), pp. 85 ff.

5. See Algot Werin, "Karaktärerna i Röda rummet," *Svenskt 1800–tal* (Lund: Gleerups, 1948), pp. 102–4.

6. Quoted in Olof Lagercrantz, "Striden om det nya riket,"

Meddelanden från Strindbergssällskapet, No. 29 (December 1961), p. 4.

7. Sven Rinman, "August Strindberg," *Ny svensk illustrerad litteraturhistoria*, 4 vols. (Stockholm: Natur & Kultur, 1957), 4:70. Eric O. Johannesson, *The Novels of August Strindberg* (Berkeley: University of California Press, 1968), pp. 55–81.

8. Quoted in Gösta Lundberg, "Fackmässig och konstnärlig exakthet i Strindbergs Hemsöborna," *Strindbergs språk och stil*, ed. Göran Lindström (Lund: Gleerups, 1964), p. 141.

9. Karl Åke Kärnell, *Strindbergs bildspråk* (Stockholm: Almqvist & Wiksell, 1962), p. 143.

10. Walter Berendsohn, *August Strindbergs skärgårds-och Stockholms-skildringar* (Stockholm: Raben & Sjögren, 1962), p. 135.

4—Sexual Warfare on the Stage

1. Carl von Linné (Linneus), a biologist and mystic who saw retributive forces at work in human life, which he called Nemesis divina. Strindberg discussed Linné's philosophy in an essay from 1887 entitled "Nemesis divina." He wrote that Linné believed "in a god's direct intervention in human life [and] . . . that the same god punishes the sinner in this life, if only in the third or fourth generation."

2. Strindberg sent his play to his editor, Albert Bonnier, who refused it. In a book of memoirs, the editor's son comments: "It was the biggest editorial mistake . . . I and my father ever made." See Gunnar Ollén, *Strindbergs dramatik* (Stockholm: Prisma, 1966), p. 130.

3. Of greater importance than the episode referred to by Strindberg was his own stay on an old estate in Denmark the year before his publication of *Miss Julie*. There he met the owner of the estate, an unmarried countess, and her steward Ludvig Hansen, a clever man who according to rumors was the countess' lover. Hansen was interested in hypnotic experiments. He made, however, a very unsympathetic impression on Strindberg, and it is possible that this led Strindberg,

who was then working on his play, to shift his sympathy to the title figure in *Miss Julie*. The episode also furnished material for Strindberg's fictional failure *Tschandala*.

4. Strindberg had found support for his negative view of women in the German writer Max Nordau, who claimed that man qua man was superior to woman. Through his strength, his more finely developed mind, and his ability to take the initiative, a man was a more genuine aristocrat than a woman, no matter how much she belonged to a social nobility.

5. Letter to Seligmann, Strindberg's German editor, October 1, 1888.

6. Maurice Valency, *The Flower and the Castle* (New York: The Macmillan Co., 1963), p. 317.

5–The Inferno Experience

1. Gunnar Brandell, *Strindbergs infernokris* (Stockholm: Bonniers, 1950).

2. Emanuel Swedenborg (1688–1772). In his early years Swedenborg pursued a program of scientific research into such areas as astronomy, mathematics, and physiology. Converted to a mystic, he began writing a number of visionary and prophetic works. However, his religious position developed from, rather than opposed his scientific research. Central to his religious philosophy was the "doctrine of correspondences," the concept that every earthly phenomenon has its counterpart in the world of the mind and the spirit. Swedenborg became crucial for a number of great writers: Blake, Goethe, Emerson, Balzac, and Yeats.

3. For a discussion of this aspect of Strindberg's Inferno crisis, see Nils Norman, "Strindberg och Dante," *Svensk litteraturtidskrift*, 3 (1964), 107.

6–Metaphysical Drama

1. Letter to his children, dated May 24, 1898.

2. Raymond Williams, *Drama from Ibsen to Eliot* (London: Chatto & Windus, 1952), p. 120.

3. John R. Milton, "The Esthetic Fault of Strindberg's 'Dream Plays,'" *Tulane Drama Review*, 4, No. 3 (1960), 108–16.

4. Evert Sprinchorn, "The Logic in A Dreamplay," *Modern Drama*, 5, No. 3 (December 1962), 342–65.

5. Sven Rinman, *Ny svensk illustrerad litteraturhistoria*, 4 vols. (Stockholm: Natur & Kultur, 1957), 4: 132.

6. Sprinchorn has pointed out that the name of Hummel might have been suggested to Strindberg by a famous case in 1905, involving an American criminal lawyer, Abraham Henry Hummel, who was convicted on charges of conspiracy. Hummel was also the name of a person who figures in Beethoven's life. See introduction to *The Chamber Plays* (New York: Dutton and Co., 1962), p. 112.

7. Barbro Ohlson, "Stora landsvägen: Önskningarnas land," *Meddelanden från Strindbergssällskapet*, No. 33 (May 1963), p. 32.

8. Quoted in Martin Lamm, *August Strindberg* (Stockholm: Aldus, 1948), p. 405.

7—Historical Dramas

1. *Open Letters to the Intimate Theatre*, trans. Walter Johnson (Seattle: University of Washington Press, 1966), p. 114.

2. Strindberg's interpretation of Hamlet anticipates Ernest Jones's Freudian analysis of the character. See *Open Letters to the Intimate Theatre*, p. 75.

3. Gunnar Ollén, *Strindbergs dramatik* (Stockholm: Prisma, 1966), p. 157.

4. *Open Letters to the Intimate Theatre*, p. 259.

5. See Ollén, *Strindbergs dramatik*, p. 195.

8—Poetry

1. Henry Olson, "Sömngångarnätter," *Synpunkter på Strindberg*, ed. Gunnar Brandell (Stockholm: Aldus, 1964), p. 134.

9—Melancholia and Militancy

1. Letter to Schering, May 6, 1907.

2. Cf. Margit Pohn, "Några bärande motiv i Svarta fanor," *Meddelanden från Strindbergssällskapet*, 29 (December 1961), 12–19, and 30–31 (May 1962), 20–29.

3. Quoted in Sven Rinman, *Ny svensk litteraturhistoria*, 4 vols. (Stockholm: Natur & Kultur, 1951), 4: 127.

10—The End and its Aftermath

1. See Sten Linder, *August Strindberg*, Verdandis småskrifter (Stockholm: Bonniers, 1948), p. 57. As a sample of Swedish reactions to Strindberg's late dramatic production one might choose the poet-reviewer Bo Bergman's impression of *The Burned House*:

Before this whipped-up soup of endless talk and platitudinous deep thoughts one caved in and would have laughed at the whole matter—if there had not been a tragic core to the play, namely the poet himself. So this is what Strindberg has come to.

2. Letter to Siri von Essen, March 1876.

Selected Bibliography

Strindberg's Works in English

For a more complete list of older translations, see Alrik Gustafson, *A History of Swedish Literature*. Minneapolis: University of Minnesota Press, 1961, pp. 651–654; and Egil Törnqvist, *Strindbergian Drama*. Stockholm: Almqvist and Wiksell International, 1982, pp. 252–54. For a more extensive bibliography, see *Strindberg: A Collection of Critical Essays*, edited by Otto Reinert, Englewood Cliffs, N.J.: Prentice-Hall, 1971, pp. 170–78, and Egil Törnqvist, *op. cit.*, 255–59.

DRAMA

Apologia and Two Folk Plays [*The Great Highway; The Crownbride; Swanwhite*]. Translated by Walter Johnson, Seattle: University of Washington Press, 1981.
The Chamber Plays by August Strindberg [*Storm Weather; The Burned House; The Ghost Sonata; The Pelican*]. Translated by Evert Springchorn and Seabury Quinn, Jr. New York: E.P. Dutton & Co., 1962.
Dramas of Testimony [*The Dance of Death I–II; Advent; Easter; There Are Crimes and Crimes*]. Translated by Walter Johnson. Seattle: University of Washington Press, 1976.
A Dreamplay. Adapted by Ingmar Bergman. Translated by Michael Meyer. London: Martin Secker & Warburg, Ltd., 1973.
A Dreamplay and Four Chamber Plays [*A Dreamplay, Stormy Weather; The House That Burned; The Ghost Sonata; The Pelican*]. Translated by Walter Johnson. Seattle: University of Washington Press, 1973.
Eight Expressionistic Plays by August Strindberg [*Lucky Per's Journey; Keys to Heaven; To Damascus I–II; A Dreamplay; Ghost Sonata; The Great Highway*]. Translated by Arvid Paulson. New York: Bantam Books, 1965.
Eight Famous Plays by Strindberg [*The Link; The Father; Miss Julie; The Stronger; There are Crimes and Crimes; Gustavus Vasa; The Dance of Death; The Spook Sonata*]. Translated by Edwin Björkman and N. Erichsen. New York and London: 1949.
Five Plays of Strindberg [*Creditors; Dance of Death; The Great Highway; Swanwhite; Crimes and Crimes*]. Translated by Elisabeth Sprigge. Garden City, N.Y.: Doubleday, 1960.
[*Historical Plays*]. 5 volumes. *Queen Christina; Charles XII; Gustaf III*, 1955. *The last of the Knights; The Regent; Earl Birger of Bjälbo*, 1956. *Gustav Adolf*, 1957. *The Saga of the Folkungs; Engelbrekt*, 1959. *The Vasa Trilogy: Master Olof, Gustav Vasa, and Erik XIV*, 1959. Translated by Walter Johnson. Seattle: University of Washington Press, 1955–1959.
Isle of the Dead. Translated by Richard Vowles. *Modern Drama*, 5, No. 3, 1962.
The Pelican. Translated by Evert Springchorn. *Tulane Drama Review*, No. 4, 1960.
The Plays. Vol. I and II [*The Father; Miss Julie; Creditors; The Stronger; Playing With Fire; Erik the Fourteenth; Storm, The Ghost Sonata*, 1964. *To Damascus I–III; Easter; The Dance of Death I–II; The Virgin Bride; A Dream Play*; 1975]. Translated by Michael Meyer. London: 1964, 1975.
Plays of Confession and Therapy [*The Dance of Death I–II; Advent; Easter; There Are Crimes and Crimes*]. Translated by Walter Johnson. Seattle: University of Washington Press, 1979.
Pre-Inferno Plays [*The Father; Miss Julie; Creditors; The Stronger; The Bond*]. Translated by Walter Johnson. Seattle: University of Washington Press, 1970.
The Road to Damascus. Translated by Graham Rawson. New York: Grove Press, 1960.
Selected Plays and Prose [*The Father; Miss Julie; Selections from Inferno; A Dreamplay*]. Edited by Robert Brustein. New York: Holt, Rinehart & Winston, 1964.
Seven Plays by Strindberg [*The Father; Miss Julie; Comrades; The Stronger; The Bond; Crimes and Crimes; Easter*]. Translated by Arvid Paulson. New York: Bantam Books, 1964.

Six Plays of Strindberg [*The Father; Miss Julie; The Stronger; Easter; A Dreamplay; The Ghost Sonata*]. Translated by Elizabeth Sprigge. Garden City, N.J.: Doubleday, 1955.

Strindberg's One-Act Plays [*The Outlaw; Miss Julie; Creditors; The Stronger; Pariah; Simoon; The First Warning; Debit and Credit; In the Face of Death; Motherlove; Playing with Fire; The Bond; The Pelican*]. Translated by Arvid Paulson. New York: Washington Square Press, 1969.

Three Experimental Plays [*Miss Julie; The Stronger; A Dream Play*]. Translated by F.R. Southerington. Charlottesville, VA.: University of Virginia Press, 1975.

Twelve Plays [*The Father; Miss Julie; Creditors; The Stronger; The Bond; Crime and Crime; Easter; The Dance of Death; Swanwhite; A Dream Play; The Ghost Sonata; The Great Highway*]. Translated by Elizabeth Sprigge. London: 1963.

World Historical Plays [*The Nightingale of Wittenberg; Through Deserts to Ancestral Lands; Hellas; The Lamb and the Beast*]. Translated by Arvid Paulson. New York: Bantam Books, 1970.

FICTION AND MISCELLANEOUS WRITING

By the Open Sea. Translated by Ellie Schleussner. London: Frank Palmer, 1913.

The Cloister. Translated by Mary Sandbach. New York: Hill & Wang, 1969.

Days of Loneliness (Ensam). Translated by Arvid Paulson. New York: Phaedra, 1971.

From an Occult Diary. Edited by Torsten Eklund. Translated by Mary Sandbach. New York: Hill & Wang, 1965.

Getting Married. Edited and translated by Mary Sandbach. New York: Viking, 1972.

Historical Miniatures. Translated by C. Field. London: George Allen & Co., Ltd. 1913.

Inferno, Alone and Other Writings (Including "The New Arts or the Role of Chance in Artistic Creation;" "Graveyard Reveries;" Jacob Wrestles"). Edited and translated by Evert Springchorn. Garden City: Doubleday, 1968.

Letters of Strindberg to Harriet Bosse. Translated by Arvid Paulson. New York: Thomas Nelson & Sons, 1959.

A Madman's Defense. Translation based on Ellie Schleussner's 1912 translation titled *Confessions of a Fool*. Introduction by Evert Springchorn. New York: Doubleday,1967.

A Madman's Manifesto. Translated by Anthony Swerling. University City, Ala.: University of Alabama Press, 1971.

The Natives of Hemso, Scapegoat. Translated by Arvid Paulson. New York: Paul S. Eriksson, 1967.

Open Letters to the Intimate Theater. Translated by Walter Johnson. Seattle: University of Washington Press, 1966.

The Red Room. Translated by Elspeth Harvey Schubert. London: Everyman, 1967.

The Son of a Servant. Translated by Evert Springchorn. Garden City, N.Y.: Doubleday, 1966.

The Strindberg Reader. (Includes Short Stories, Essays, Poetry). Translated and edited by Arvid Paulson. New York: Phaedra, 1968.

Tales. Translated by L.J. Potts. London: George Allen & Co., Ltd., 1930.

Zones of the Spirit: A Book of Thoughts. (Contains excerpts from The Blue Books). Translated and edited by C. Field. London: George Allen & Co., Ltd., 1913.

English Works on Strindberg

BOOKS (including chapters in books on modern drama and special Strindberg issues of literary journals).

Anderson, Hans. *Strindberg's Master Olof and Shakespeare*. Cambridge, Mass.: Harvard University Press, 1952.

Bentley, Eric. *The Playwright as Thinker*. New York: Meridian Books, 1960, pp. 193–215.

–––. *In Search of Theater*. New York: Knopf, 1953, pp. 134–43.

Brandell, Gunnar. *Strindberg in Inferno*. Translated from the Swedish by Barry Jacobs. Cambridge. Mass.: Harvard University Press, 1974.

Brustein, Robert. *The Theatre of Revolt*. Boston: Little, Brown & Co., 1964, pp. 87–134.

Carlson, Harry G. *Strindberg and Myth*. Berkeley: University of California Press, 1982.

Dahlström, Carl. *Strindberg's Dramatic Expressionism*. Ann Arbor: University of Michigan Press, 1930.

Essays on Strindberg. Edited by Carl R. Smedmark. Stockholm: J. Beckman for the Strindberg Society, 1966.

Grant, Vernon W. *Great Abnormals: The Pathological Genius of Kafka, van Gogh, Strindberg and Poe*. New York: Hawthorne Books, 1968.

Gustafson, Alrik. *A History of Swedish Literature*. Minneapolis: University of Minnesota Press, 1961, pp. 243–87.

Johannesson, Eric O. *The Novels of August Strindberg*. Berkeley: University of California Press, 1963.

Johnson, Walter. *August Strindberg*. Boston: Twayne (TWAS 410), 1978.

– – –. *Strindberg and the Historical Drama*. Seattle: University of Washington Press, 1963.

Klaf, Franklin S. *The Origin of Psychology in Modern Drama*. New York: The Citadel Press, 1963.

Lamm, Martin. *Modern Drama*. Translated by Karin Elliott. Oxford: Philosophical Library, 1952, pp. 135–51.

– – –. *August Strindberg*. Translated and edited by Harry G. Carlson. New York: B. Blom, 1971.

Lagercrantz, Olof. *August Strindberg*. English translation forthcoming of Swedish edition printed in 1979 [Stockholm: Wahlström & Widstrand].

Lucas, F.L. *The Drama of Ibsen and Strindberg*. New York: MacMillan Co., 1963.

Madsen, Børge Gedsø. *Strindberg's Naturalistic Theatre*. Seattle: University of Washington Press, 1962.

Modern Drama 5, No. 3, 1962. Special Strindberg issue edited by Robert Shedd.

Mortensen, Brita and Brian Downs. *Strindberg: An Introduction to His Life and Work*. Cambridge: Cambridge University Press, 1949.

Sprigge, Elizabeth. *The Strange Life of August Strindberg*. London: Chatto & Windus, 1949.

Strindberg. A Collection of Essays. Edited by Otto Reinert. Twentieth Century Views. Englewood Cliffs, N.J.: Prentice-Hall, 1971.

Strindbergs Dramen im Lichte neuerer Methodendiskussion. Basel: Helbring & Lichtenhahn, 1981. Contains several articles in English.

Structures of Influence. A Comparative Approach to August Strindberg. Festskrift to Walter Johnson. Edited by Marilyn Johns Blackwell. Chapel Hill: University of North Carolina Press, 1981.

Swerling, Anthony. *Strindberg's Impact in France 1920–1960*. Cambridge: Cambridge University Press, 1971.

The Unknown Strindberg. Edited by Harry G. Carlson. Special Strindberg issue, *Scandinavian Review*, 64 (Sept.) 1976.

ARTICLES

Adler, Henry. "To Hell with Society." *Tulane Drama Review* 4 (May, 1960), 53–76.

Allen, James L., Jr. "Symbol and Meaning in *Crime and Crime*." *Modern Drama*, 9 (1966), 62–73.

Brandy, Stephen C. "Strindberg's Biblical Sources for *The Ghost Sonata*." *Scandinavian Studies*, 40 (1968), 200–209.

Bentson, Alice N. "From Naturalism to the *Dream Play*: A Study of the Evolution of Strindberg's Unique Theatrical Form." *Modern Drama*, 7 (1963), 382–98.

Bentley, Eric. "The Ironic Strindberg." In Springchorn, Evert, ed. *The Genius of the Scandinavian Theater*. New York: New American Library, 1964, pp.599–603.

Bergeron, David M. "Strindberg's Easter. A Musical Play." *University Review* (Kansas City, University of Missouri), 33 (1967), 219–22.

Bergholz, Harry. "Strindberg's Anthologies of American Humorists, Bibliographically Identified." *Scandinavian Studies*, 43 (1971), 335–43.

Bronsen, David. "The Dance of Death and the Possibility of Laughter." *Drama Survey* 6 (1967), 31–44.

Carlson, Harry G. "Ambiguity and Archetypes in Strindberg's *Romantic Organist*." *Scandinavian Studies*, 48 (1976), 256–71.

Dear, Irving, "Strindberg's Dream Vision: Prelude to Film" *Criticism*, 14 (1972), 253–65.

De Paul, Brother C.F.X. "Bergman and Strindberg: Two Philosophies of Suffering." *College English*, 26 (1965), 620–30.

Flaxman, Seymour L. "The Debt of Williams and Miller to Ibsen and Strindberg." *Comparative Literature Studies* (Special Advance Issue, 1963), pp. 51–60.

Fletcher, John, "Bergman and Strindberg." *Journal of Modern Literature*, 3 (1973), 173–90.

Freedman, Morris. "Strindberg's Positive Nililism." In Freedman, Morris, ed. *Essays in the Modern Drama*. (Boston: Heath, 1964), pp. 56–63. Reprinted from *Drama Survey*, 2 (1963), 288–96.

Hamilton, Mary G. "Strindberg's Alchemical Way of the Cross." *Mosaik* 7:4 (Summer 1974), pp. 139–53.

Hartman, Murray. "Strindberg and O'Neill." *Educational Theatre Journal*, 18:3 (Oct. 1966), pp. 216–31.

Hauptman, Ira. "Strindberg's Realistic Plays." *Yale Theatre*, 5:2 (1974), pp. 87–94.

Hays, Stephen G. and Jules Zentner. "Strindberg's *Miss Julie*: Lilacs and Beer." *Scandinavian Studies*, 45 (1973), 59–64.

Hildeman, Karl-Ivar, "Strindberg, *The Dance of Death* and Revenge." *Scandinavian Studies*, 25 (1963), 267–94.

Holtan, Orley I. "The Absurd World of Strindberg's *The Dance of Death*." *Comparative Drama*, 1 (1967), 199–206.

Jarvi, Raymond. "Strindberg's *The Ghost Sonata* and Sonata Form." *Mosaic*, 5:4 (Summer 1972), pp. 69–84.

———. "Ett drömspel: A Symphony for the Stage." *Scandinavian Studies*, 44 (1972) 28–42.

Johns, Marilyn. "Journey into Autumn: *Oväder* and *Smultronstället*." *Scandinavian Studies*, 50 (1978), 133–49.

———. "Strindberg's *Folkungasagan* and Bergman's *Det sjunde inseglet*: Medieval Epic and Psychological Drama." *Scandinavica* 27:1 (May 1979), pp. 21–34.

Johnson, Walter. "*Gustaf Adolf* Revised." *Scandinavian Studies for Henry Goddard Leach*. Seattle: University of Washington Press, 1965, pp. 236–46.

Kauffman, K.J. "Strindberg: The Absence of Irony." *Drama Survey*, 3 (1964), 463–76.

Kaufman, Michael W. "Strindberg's Historical Imagination: Erik XIV." *Comparative Drama*, 9 (1975–76), 318–31.

Lapisardi, Frederick S. "The Same Enemies: Notes in Certain Similarities between Yeats and Strindberg." *Modern Drama*, 12 (1969), 146–54.

Lawson, Stephen R. "Strindberg's *Dream Play* and *Ghost Sonata*." *Yale Theatre*, 5:2 (1974), 95–102.

Lewis, Leta Jane. "Alchemy and the Orient in Strindberg's *Dream Play*." *Scandinavian Studies*, 35 (1963), 208–22.

Lide, Barbara. "Strindberg and Moliere: Parallels, Influence, Image." *Moliere and the Commonwealth of Letters: Patrimony and Posterity*. Jackson, Miss.: Mississippi University Press, 1975.

Lyons, Charles R. "Archetypal Action of Male Submission in Strindberg's *The Father*." *Scandinavian Studies*, 36 (1964), 218–32.

McNamara, Brooks. "Scene Design: 1876–1965. Ibsen, Chechov, Strindberg." *Tulane Drama Review*, 13:2 (T42), (Winter 1968), pp. 77–91.

Mays, Milton A. "Strindberg's *Ghost Sonata*: Parodied Fairy Tale on Original Sin." *Modern Drama*, 10 (1967), 189–94.

Parker, Gerald. "The Spectator Seized by the Theatre: Strindberg's *The Ghost Sonata*." *Modern Drama*, 15 (1972), 373–86.

Plasberg, Elaine. "Strindberg and the New Poetics." *Modern Drama*, 15 (1972), 1–14.

Scobbie, Irene. "Strindberg and Lagerkvist." *Modern Drama*, 7 (1964), 126–34.

Senelick, Lawrence. "Strindberg, Antoine and Lugné-Poë: A Study in Cross Purposes." *Modern Drama*, 15 (1973), 391–402.

Springchorn, Evert. "Strindberg and Greater Naturalism." *Tulane Drama Review*, 13:2 (Winter 1968), pp. 119–29.

———. "The Zola of the Occult: Strindberg's Experimental Method." *Modern Drama*, 17 (1974), 250–66.

———. "Hell and Purgatory in Strindberg." *Scandinavian Studies*, 50 (1978), 371–80.

Steene, Birgitta. "The Ambiguous Feminist." *Scandinavian Review*, 64:3 (Sept. 1976), pp. 27–31.

———. "Shakespearean Elements in Historical Plays of Strindberg." *Comparative Literature* 11 (1959), 209–20.

Stockenström, Göran. "The Journey from the Isle of Life to the Isle of the Dead: The Idea of Reconciliation in *The Ghost Sonata*." *Scandinavian Studies*, 50 (1978), 133–49.

Syndergaard, Larry E. "The *Skogsrå* of Folklore and Strindberg's *The Crown Bride*." *Comparative Drama*, 6 (1972–73), 310–22.

Törnqvist, Egil. "Strindberg's *The Stronger*." *Scandinavian Studies*, 42 (1970), 297–308.

———. "*Miss Julie* and O'Neill." *Modern Drama*, 19 (1976), 351–64.

Warme, Lars G. "Translations as Distorted Mirrors. Strindberg Redivivus." *Canadian Review of Comparative Literature*, (Spring 1980), pp. 183–95.

The student is also advised to check *Scandinavian Studies*, 13 (1951) for an extensive bibliography by Esther H. Rapp, listing English and American scholarship on Strindberg up to 1950. The *Modern Drama* special Strindberg issue 5, (1962) contains an extension of Rapp's bibliography by Jackson R. Bryer. These two bibliographies in turn are updated by Birgitta Steene in *Structures of Influence. A Comparative Approach to August Strindberg*. Festskrift to Walter Johnson. Chapel Hill, N.C.: University of North Carolina Press, 1982, pp. 256–76.